Surviving the System

The Story of the Santa Shooter

Surviving the System: The Story of the Santa Shooter
Marcus Allen Weldon
Copyright © 2017 by Marcus Weldon

ISBN: 978-0-9989239-2-5

Published by True Vine Publishing Co.
P.O. Box 22448
Nashville, TN. 37202
www.TrueVinePublishing.org

Cover Design by: Delynea Blessett
Illustrator Daniel Coney @dconeyart

Printed in the United States of America

All rights reserved. No part of this book may be reproduced or transmitted in any form or by any means, electronic or mechanical, including photocopy, recording, or by any information storage and retrieval system with the exception of a reviewer who may quote brief passages in a review to be printed in a newspaper or magazine without permission from the author.

This is a true story. The names and identifying details have been changed to protect the privacy of individuals.

Contact author at:
www.MarcusWeldon.com
Facebook: Marcus Allen Weldon
Youtube: Marcus Allen Weldon
Instagram: Marcus_allen_weldon

Surviving the System

The Story of the Santa Shooter

Marcus Allen Weldon

www.TrueVinePublishing.org
Nashville, TN

TABLE OF CONTENTS

Acknowledgements 7
Introduction 9
Chapter 1: The Day Before 13
Chapter 2: What Really Happened? 22
Chapter 3: Welcome to the County 34
Chapter 4: Never Ride 4-Deep 52
Chapter 5: Media Blitz 66
Chapter 6: Not the Judge, Too?! 80
Chapter 7: House Arrest 100
Chapter 8: Alcohol, Shoes, and Books 110
Chapter 9: How Did I Get Here? 127
Chapter 10: I Actually Learned Something in School 146
Chapter 11: The Trial 167
Chapter 12: Father's Day Weekend 193
Chapter 13: The Verdict is In 205
Appendix— Authors and Books that Influenced Me

ACKNOWLEDGEMENTS

I want to thank God for getting me through this tough time and keeping me level-headed and strong. I thank God for forgiving me for when I was wrong, but I know He didn't give up on me.

I thank my mother for being a warrior in the courtroom and coming to every single court date and not missing a beat! You were always loving. THANK YOU!

I thank my Dad for instilling a good work ethic in me, for building me up to be the man I am today and sticking with me through the entire process.

I thank my daughter, Za'Nya, for being my inspiration! You were the reason I didn't give up!

I thank my brother, Lil' Aaron. I called on your strength as well. Stay strong. God will get you through anything!

I thank my girlfriend, Delynea, for putting up with my mess! I haven't been perfect, but you loved me anyway through thick and thin. I love you!

I thank my pastor, Alonzo Bell, and the Martin Evans Missionary Baptist Church family. You all showed up and showed out! You were the ultimate prayer warriors in the heat of the battle.

I thank my cousin, Ted, for giving me a chance to learn about how real business gets done! Got 'em!

Thank you, Mr. and Mrs. Flowers, for being a second family and coming to court with me.

Thank you, Curtis, for being a brother from another mother!

I thank my boy, Juan, for you-know-what!

I thank all of my co-workers who became more than colleagues, but family. You know who you are!

I thank C. J. Grisham for helping me throughout this journey. Thank you for helping out a stranger!

I thank Rick Ector for going above and beyond just being legal counsel, but also being a friend.

Thank you, Attorney David Cripps, for putting up the good fight!

I thank Tiffanie Y. Lewis for, not only being my Book Coach, but keeping me focused throughout the whole process of writing this book. Thank you for believing in my story!

Thank you Dre, Patrice Baker, Brian Banks, Gary and Dee Bradfield, Joi, Odell Tate, Chris, Lil' Joe, Terrence Council, the Jury, and Officer Ray Randolph!! R.I.P. Wymon and Rome – I know you were with me in court!

I appreciate everyone one who called, texted, and commented on social media. Your love and support means more to me than I can ever express!

INTRODUCTION

See It Through
By: Edger Albert Guest

When you're up against a trouble,
Meet it squarely, face to face;
Lift your chin and set your shoulders,
Plant your feet and take a brace.
When it's vain to try to dodge it,
Do the best that you can do;
You may fail, but you may conquer,
See it through!

Black may be the clouds about you
And your future may seem grim,
But don't let your nerve desert you;
Keep yourself in fighting trim.
If the worst is bound to happen,
Spite of all that you can do,
Running from it will not save you,
See it through!

Even hope may seem but futile,
When with troubles you're beset,
But remember you are facing
Just what other men have met.

> *You may fail, but fall still fighting;*
> *Don't give up, whate'er you do;*
> *Eyes front, head high to the finish.*
> *See it through!*

I've had an interesting journey throughout my short life. I've lost friends to street violence and others I had to cut loose in order to find myself – my true self. Never was it in my plan to write a book. Some may consider it an autobiography of the earlier stages of my life, but I consider it personal memoirs-- life lessons told in a story-like format and placed in a book. It contains the highest of highs and the lowest of lows in my life, which prepared me to face off with one of the most challenging situations that Black men face in America. The challenge of an innocent man fighting through the corrupt and unpredictable jaws of the justice system.

In 2014, I gained full custody of my 6-year-old daughter. I participated on Detroit Mayor Mike Duggan's Recreational Advisory Board. I was mentoring young men through a program with the former Detroit Mayor, Dave Bing. I was in school learning to be a building engineer. In my spare time, I would teach kids hands-on applications of skilled trades through a non-profit organization called *Redeem Detroit*. I was earning respect in the community and being the responsible citizen I thought every young man should be.

After a long night working at a Christmas fundraiser, a friend of mine and I had an encounter with two men that has changed my life completely. The media and the courts had gotten this case all wrong, but, of course, it was up to me and my defense to prove it.

CHAPTER 1
The Day Before

"While Detroit is witnessing a paradoxical resurgence between downtown and Midtown (commercial corridor), amounting to billions of dollars in investment, the city's neighborhoods (urban corridor), which comprise more than 82.7 percent African-Americans and 32,490 Black-owned businesses, have largely been ignored for any economic opportunities, resources and benefits."

– Ken Harris, Michigan Black Chamber of Commerce President and CEO

The sound of voices and sirens was all I could hear as I laid on the cold, black gravel. My face was pressed up against the broken asphalt in front of St. Andrews nightclub. The cold hard steel of the handcuffs digging into my wrist felt like teeth from a pit bull.

My brain was stained with the scary images of me firing my black semi-automatic 40-caliber pistol at a human being. Of course, those images were mixed with emotions as I thought of my 5-year-old daughter, who I'd just won full custody of almost a year ago. How did I go from working on my plan to spend my first Christmas with her, to being dressed as Santa Claus and possibly killing someone?

My Adam's apple was stuck in my throat and my tongue was so dry that the asphalt and it had more in common with each other than I did with this harsh reality. "What just happened?" I asked myself, as the crowd in front of St. Andrews took pictures of my lifeless-looking body wrapped up in a Santa Claus suit like a Christmas package. However, this wasn't how my weekend started. As a matter fact, it was totally the opposite!

I had come a long way. Never in a million years would I have thought I would be working with political figures in Detroit. I was blessed to be appointed by Detroit Mayor Mike Duggan's Recreational Advisory Board. I was now in a position where I could truly change lives in Detroit, while working alongside city council members, state representatives and district leaders of the city.

Being a member of the Board would give me the opportunity to voice my opinion, give ideas and advice to the Mayor's Organization on recreating our city. I saw myself becoming the voice of the community to the mayor through the advisory board. I've come a long way and I certainly don't look like what I've been through.

After a 4-year court battle, I gained full custody of my daughter, defining the true example of a single, "Black Father," which is the opposite of the stereotypical "Baby Daddies" the television and media loves to portray. My daughter's mother had an alcohol and drug problem. It was a spiral effect that brought me down spiritually, mentally, and physically.

This battle left me depressed, defeated and helpless, but after the battle was won, it fortified my character and I felt like a new man! This was great because this would be my first Christmas that I would have my daughter with me. My ex would usually have my daughter on Christmas Eve because she would have our daughter on major holidays.

I also began to pursue modeling and signed a contract with a company called *SoHo* which did promotions for well-known liquor companies. They would send me to various locations like liquor stores, clubs, and concerts to promote their brand as a liquor ambassador. I would sometimes also be the AV Tech whose job was to set up events with banners and lights.

I even worked as a photographer, taking pictures and videos at the events. This taught me the basic skills of marketing and event planning. I learned how to target direct audiences, develop my social skills, and counter market competitors who offered similar products. It also lead me into more lucrative promotional opportunities with liquor promos and other marketing companies.

Along with my job for the liquor company, I also worked with my cousin, Theodore Lagarde. He had a new patented pet product called the Laguard Fitness Vest. The Laguard Vest is the highest quality training and exercise apparatus for dogs that exists. It is a black-owned and Michigan-based product. The vest aids in building muscle and strength in pets during exercise and it helps to increase stamina and endurance.

In this job I exercised my marketing skills and used them to master social media branding. I was brought along to meetings with possible big investors of the product. I quickly learned how to present myself in meetings, how to talk, dress, and speak financial rhetoric. This was the beginning of my entrepreneurial mindset. I was slowly becoming a "polymathic" entrepreneur, someone who learns a lot in many fields of study. I learned that word while reading a book on Benjamin Franklin.

I was featured on the news in Detroit twice for something good in 2014, on both Fox 2 and Channel 7 television stations. Once, I was a promotional model for Detroit Dog Rescue's K9 Couture fashion show on Fox. The "K9 Couture" was a fashion show held at the Townsend Hotel in Birmingham, Michigan, which featured fashion models on the runway along with their dogs wearing new clothes and exposing new pet products to the local market. It was an opportunity that gave me some exposure, which I needed with my up and coming modeling career.

Another time, I was on the news with my Pastor Alonzo Bell, of Martin Evans Missionary Baptist Church, who was featured on Channel 7 for taking action in reviving the city through his non-profit organization Redeem Detroit. I was acknowledged as one of his mentees. He was given the Channel 7 20/20 Action award along with $7,000 in cash to help his mission. Redeem Detroit's mission is to rehabilitate vacant buildings and properties in the neighborhoods and open businesses in them.

They also focus on training at-risk youth, homeless veterans, and returning citizens (from prison) in vocational and job readiness skills. The intention is that with these skills, the participants can help clean up the neighborhood and find job opportunities.

My accolades were building up. Now, as if all of this wasn't enough, I was also a part time student at Wayne County Community College and full-time building engineer at a casino. I was hustling! When I went through the custody battle with my daughter's mother, it changed me. I began thinking, "I gotta do something… I gotta make something of my life because I got a baby girl to take care of."

As a father, I was a protector. When you have a child, a daughter in particular, it changes your outlook on life. It makes you think twice before disrespecting a woman. It matured me as a young man and molded me into a role model for all young fathers. I would get asked for advice constantly from single fathers. They would ask questions like, "How did you get custody, man?" and "What attorney did you use?" or "What did you have to do?" I saw Black men who really wanted to be fathers. The interest was there.

Relationships can go bad, but it should never come between you and your child. A good father follows what I call the "Three Rules of Fatherhood": Provide, nurture and guide. It is a problem when a man doesn't see himself as being legitimate or if he sees himself as being inadequate. If you are a father and feel like you can't follow any of these fatherhood rules, you might sometimes back out of your children's lives. You may be afraid or disgusted with yourself, but you don't have to be.

I didn't want to be one of those parents who didn't leave anything for their children when they're gone.

I wanted to be a good role model. I want my baby girl to be comfortable asking me how to do things because she could see me being successful. When I fell out with her mother, I felt like I had to prove to her that I could make something of myself. I used this as a motivation. My daughter kept me going.

I didn't want to get satisfied with just doing enough to get by. I really felt like I could change the world and give a different perspective of a Black man and his willingness to fight for his child. The truth is that a lot of young men don't know how to go about fighting for their daughters, and I learned a lot about how to do it right, but that's another story for another day.

My experiences up to this point from *Redeem Detroit* and a few years of school allowed me to step up from the housekeeping department and into the engineering department. This opened the doors for growth in the company because the more education I got, the more money I could make! I was determined to finish my 4-year degree at Wayne State University, officially graduate, and then give back by teaching kids in the Redeem program the same skills I acquired.

Six days before Christmas, I was invited to be at Brenda Jones holiday celebration in downtown Detroit. Brenda Jones was initially elected to serve the citizens as a city councilperson in 2005. On January 6, 2014, Ms. Jones was elected President of the Detroit City Council. The excitement about the party and my opportunities flowed through my body. I felt like a kid at a carnival getting his first elephant ear. I was in a position to really make my mark on the "who's who" of the political world and draw attention to the issues at hand in our community.

Detroit had a lot of issues to handle including the lack of lucrative job opportunities for the citizens of the Detroit. In my opinion, any new big businesses in the city needs to hire the more people in the inner city first before going out and hiring people from the outside. We also need programs to re-educate our kids on finances and teach them how to start their own businesses and learning the value of acquiring money management skills.

I felt we needed to feel more comfortable when talking about racism and culture. My intention was not to create or exacerbate a race war, but instead to excavate a lost history and culture. This would ameliorate some of the conscious and unconscious inferiority complexes that African-Americans have in Detroit. It would boost their confidence and let them know that even in these impoverished circumstances, you are not a mistake. Through programs like Redeem Detroit we can accomplish this.

It's not just about the color of the masses either, but instead, the division of the poor and working classes. Detroit is just over 80 percent black and close to 17 percent Latino and White. Since almost half of Detroit's population is under the poverty level this affects the city as a whole. We are all children of God, but in this capitalist democracy, it seems to me that the government has put money and power over the well-being of humanity. This is one of the community's major concerns.

The community also had questions on what was being done to tackle blight. The neighborhoods are desolated in some areas. "Is the government focusing only on certain areas that they feel are important? Why are they shutting off people's water in the neighborhoods but these big businesses get away with owing thousands of dollars?" were questions I asked myself. I was interested in raising my concerns on these and other issues and this party seemed like just the place to do it.

Everyone was there from city council members, to district managers and even the Mayor himself. The stage was set. I had the perfect suit on. It was a tailored all-black suit with the red dress shirt and black tie from Express along with the black Cole Haan Loafers. This was the same suit I wore on Fox 2 News for the fashion show. It was not too loud, but just enough red to bring the outfit alive. I had intentions of running for office one day in the future and I had to be presentable in every way possible. This was my first chance to make a good impression.

My agenda was set to help the African-American youth of the city—an agenda on which most politicians of the city never focus. I thought I could be the poster child for someone who benefits from positive city programs and the city could bring more constructive programs to the table. I was going to lead by example.

All my accomplishments led up to this point. I was out to show the world that Black men aren't all thugs and those who had difficult and criminal pasts could turn the corner and come back from it. If only national news could focus on the good stories in Detroit, like mine, and so many others.

Now, you can't have a party without food! They served pasta and chicken for dinner and a chocolate cake for dessert that lasted all of 30 minutes before I devoured it like I hadn't eaten in 3 days. After dinner, I discussed ideas of mentorship programs with some local community leaders and they were impressed with some of the things I was suggesting. The lack of young people stepping up was common.

Suddenly, everyone's attention seemed to shift to the entrance of the room. Mayor Mike Duggan had just walked in the room and everyone's energy level raised to another level. You could see the anticipation of his arrival with all of the people's body language.

Mayor Duggan had on a gray suit on with a white button up shirt like normal. I took a picture with him and told him I was excited about being on the Recreational Advisory Board. He smiled and said, "Thank you for volunteering and taking pride in your city." I was starting to become a familiar face among the district representatives and city council members. This was the fourth or fifth time I was able to rub elbows with the Mayor. My life was at its peak, but it's crazy how things can change in the blink of an eye.

CHAPTER 2
What Really Happened

"We as men should stand up as men and protect our women and children. I am a man, and I will walk upright as a man should. I will not crawl."

– Robert F. Williams, 1959 NAACP Convention

Things started off well, like most Saturdays. I had a quick trip to the gym and the barbershop before I got started on my liquor promos. On a normal promotion, I would be in a suit and the ladies I worked with would be in dresses, but the liquor company had something else in store for Christmas.

The liquor company had a great event coming up at a club in downtown Detroit. It was a Christmas party featuring Santa Claus and his female helpers. My manager decided to have me dress as Santa Claus and all of my female coworkers would dress as Mrs. Claus. I would have been a little embarrassed to be dressed in a silly outfit, but the pay was amazing. *"$300 for three hours? Not bad for a side hustle!"* I thought to myself.

I was the AV Tech that night as well as Santa, so I had to be at the event early to set up. My barber was also throwing a party at his shop for Christmas and he wanted me to show up to his party as Santa. It would have added a little Christmas flavor to his party. I agreed to make an appearance after I left work, but my focus was on the Christmas party at the club.

I know you're wondering how I pulled off looking like Santa. With my slim frame, we bear no resemblance at all. Well, for starters, I wore three layers of clothes under my red Santa suit, which included three shirts and a North Face ® coat. Also, I had on the full white beard, a red hat and black overall boots that went over my shoes. I was extremely hot and had to stay hydrated, so I drank plenty of water throughout the night.

The party was exhilarating and the crowd was thick at the club, which it always was on a Saturday night. People loved the sight of me in a Santa Claus suit. They compared me to the Santa Claus on Ice Cube's movie "Friday After Next". I was a skinny Black Santa Claus, but instead of robbing people, I was surrounded by women dressed in skimpy Mrs. Claus outfits. It was kind of funny now that I think about it.

Of course, everyone wanted to take pictures on Santa's lap. I was the star of the show and was loving it. I made fun out of an uncomfortable situation. It kept me motivated… along with those skimpy dresses! You feel me? Say what you want, but Santa was doing his thing and no one could say anything differently.

The music at the party was crazy and the radio station, 95.5 FM (Channel 955), blasted it on the air all night. Friends came through to show me love and, of course, laugh at me. It was all in good fun and helped pass the time.

I had the other event on my mind and needed to save as much energy as possible. My plan was to leave about 1 o'clock or 1:15 a.m. and head to the barber shop. I also had to stop at another club around the corner to pick up some promotional giveaways for my next event.

As time winded down, one of my co-workers dressed as Mrs. Claus, Jasmine, came to me and said, "Let's clean up now so we can be ready to go at one." She wanted to go to another party afterwards herself. As the night ended, I helped Jasmine load her car up with the leftover liquor company merchandise.

While loading the car, Jasmine noticed her tire on the front passenger side was low. We contemplated if she could make it home or to her next destination on this low tire. I was already late for my next stop and so was she. I told her I had to make a quick stop downtown and then I was off to my barber's Christmas party. I didn't feel she could make it so I told her, "Go to the Speedway on Jefferson and I'll meet you there to put the air in for you."

I was reluctant to go and, in hindsight, I should have sent a tow truck driver to assist her instead. I was trying to do too much and at the same time be a chivalrous Santa. The time of night was not the right time to be changing tires. Certain parts of Detroit are dangerous places at the wrong time of day and, well, as they say, you should always follow your first mind.

After a quick stop to pick up more supplies from the PV lounge, Jasmine called me and said that she was pulling into the gas station. I told her I was three minutes away and around 1:21 a.m. I pulled up to the station.

When I saw a hole in the tire about the size of my thumb, I knew my thought of this being a quick fix was out of the window.

Unfortunately, Jasmine didn't have a jack. *"This is going to be hard again,"* I thought to myself. It seemed like every time I needed to change a tire, it was always an arduous task. "Nothing can ever be easy!" I mentally yelled to myself. It's always the hard way in my life and this was no different from my normal tire changing experiences.

I had to think about what I could do next, considering that it was getting late and we were looking like a quick lick to any thieves or kidnappers. A man in a baggy Santa suit with a woman in a skimpy Mrs. Claus dress at 1:30 a.m was not exactly intimidating. We were looking like a couple of sheep among wolves.

Since there was no jack, I had to call a tow truck. As I dialed the number I noticed that Jasmine had left the car and walked over to the gas station's window to purchase something. *"Typical stupid blonde move. Never wander off this time of the night,"* I thought to myself. Now, as a man, I couldn't let her go to the window by herself this late. It wasn't in my upbringing to do so. I had to go check on her to make sure she was ok. I grabbed my gun from the car and headed towards Jasmine.

As I approached the window I noticed a black car about fifteen feet away from her with the passenger door wide open. The driver was still in the car, and the passenger of the car was standing about a foot away from Jasmine, but facing his buddy in the car.

The passenger looked like he was about 5 feet, 8 inches tall and 185 lbs. He seemed to be of Middle Eastern descent and he was dressed in all black. He was talking back and forth with the driver in a Middle Eastern language. *"Nothing odd about that,"* I thought, until the strangest thing happened.

The Middle Eastern male started pushing Jasmine for no reason. I couldn't understand why he would push her. It looked as if he was trying to initiate an altercation of some sort. She did nothing to him at all. I wondered, "Is he drunk? Or maybe he's trying to set up some type of distraction to rob us," which is a common strategy for robbers in the D. "Is he trying to snatch Jasmine?" Human trafficking was a heavy problem around the world and growing in Detroit, too.

I couldn't tell what his motives were, but I could tell that he wasn't in his right mind. He was angry and his eyes were blood shot red. His speech was a little slurred like he was high off something. Chills went down my spine, and I started to feel that feeling that you get when you're not sure what's about to happen, but you know it's not good. The ambiguity and suspense was killing me and my mind was racing with pessimistic thoughts.

Jasmine screamed, "Why did you push me?" as the man quickly closed in on her. He replied, "I didn't touch you!" and got less than six inches away from Jasmine's face yelling. I couldn't understand why he seemed impervious to the fact that I was standing right there beside them watching the whole thing. He simply ignored the fact that there was someone with this young lady. I could have easily been her husband, brother or whomever. This was so disrespectful!

I guess he didn't think I would step up and intervene. Was this Santa suit that unintimidating to the point where he could try two strangers at a gas station at night? In Detroit? I had to say something. "Hey bro! Chill out, leave her alone!" I yelled. The man looked at me and said, "The fuck you gonna do, Santa?" Then, he charged at me with the look of the devil in his eyes. In a blink of an eye, the situation got uglier and uglier.

He pushed me in my chest. I could feel my gun on my waistline slipping. The pants were entirely too big and three layers of clothes under the suit restricted my mobility. The Santa pants began to fall. Quickly, with my right hand, I pushed him in the face to get him off of me. I could tell that made him angrier.

He yelled to his partner in the car once again speaking in his native tongue. I started thinking, "Why would he change back to this foreign tongue? He clearly spoke English before, so he must be trying to relay some type of coded message to his partner for back up. The passenger door was wide open and I saw that his partner was scrambling between the seats looking for something.

I stepped back and put my hand on the pistol by my side, fearing for my life and said, "Hold up! I'm warning you to get back and leave us alone." By this time my heart was racing and I didn't know if the driver was going to start shooting, so I had to watch him and his crazy buddy who was still looking for a fight.

The man looked down at my weapon, unintimidated, and made no concession to my warning. I could tell he didn't believe I had it in me to shoot. He said to me, "I got something for you nigga!" and raced back to the open car door. He began reaching into the car to his partner. "Shit is about to get real," I said as I contemplated what to do next. *"He's getting a gun and if I don't think fast this could be it for me and Jasmine."*

"Now, how did it get to this point here? Did he not respect a Black woman or man that much, that he felt that he could say and do whatever he wanted with no repercussions? Was I supposed to bow down to him and not stand up for the young lady?" All of this was running through my head as the man turned back towards me with a Black pistol in his hand. He started walking towards me in an aggressive manner. "Jasmine run!" I yelled, as I began to back up, never taking my eyes off him.

In a split second, my life was about to change. I was going to have to make the hardest decision in my life. Suddenly, he pointed the gun at me and everything slowed down like it did in "The Matrix." I felt like Neo when he was being attacked by multiple agents and had to focus. Everything seemed so slow, but it was the opposite; I was just moving so fast, just like Neo.

Imagine yourself in my shoes. A guy gets his gun and starts to come towards you. He begins to raise his arm and points the gun at you. What do you do? There is no real-life training for this. It's just pure instincts and adrenaline where any second could be your last second alive.

I pointed my gun at him and focused on his chest area and fired. Then, he returned fire, the sounds of overlapping gun fire bounced off the walls of the gas station. Each shot could have easily pierced a gas pump igniting a fire and killing us all.

I continued to fire shots as I backed up, I wasn't even sure if my aim was as accurate as my imagination seemed to be making it out to be. I mean, the guy was still standing and moving along the vehicle in a horizontal shooting position, looking bullet proof. We were now in a full Wild, Wild West shoot out!

Each shot from my gun had a louder echo than the last one. I remember staring at the barrel of my gun watching every shell eject from the top of the chamber. I had shot this gun at moving targets before at the range, but never at moving people. It was a different ball game now.

I heard shots coming from the black car. *"Was the driver shooting at me, too? Were there two guns in the car?"* I fired my last shots, and then I ran after Jasmine who had already taken off before the shootout began.

As I continued to fire and backup simultaneously, I remember there being a light at the gas station shining brightly down on me like God had opened the sky. With the noises of gun fire sounding like 4th of July bottle rockets whizzing past me, I wonder if that was actually God putting his hand around me protecting me from being hit.

Screams from Jasmine snapped me out of the trance I was in. I ran to make sure she was alright. Naturally, my mind was imagining the worst, like Jasmine being shot in the back and, seconds later, falling face first into the concrete after the initial shock of being shot wore off. But that's not what happened.

Jasmine ran into the middle of the street, almost getting hit by a moving car. The force of the moving vehicle almost knocked her to her knees. Frantically, she smacked the moving car's windows with her hands yelling for them to stop their car and help us. I grabbed her by the arm and pull her back to see if she was hurt. At the same time, I grabbed my phone and began to call 911.

My hand was shaking and I kept dialing the wrong number. At first, 9-1-7. Then, 9-1-6…9-1-5 and then finally on my fourth attempt, my trembling thumb hit that last infamous digit…9-1-1. The 911 operator answered the line and I began to tell them that I needed help, but it was too much going on for me to give them details like our location. I was scared too, but I realized I had to keep my composure together in order to make sure we both made it out of this alive.

Then, I realized that it wasn't over yet. It was a strong possibility that the two threats were not dead. I turned back around to see if we were being followed. Surprisingly, we were being followed by a black car that looked just like the one I just had a shootout with. I hung up on the 911 operator abruptly. It was time to run for cover and possibly prepare for round two of this shootout. My life became a Christmas edition James Bond movie before my eyes!

I saw an alley up ahead and I knew that if I could get behind a dumpster or wall, we might be able to hold these guys off a little longer before police arrived. I recognized that they were hurt, but I just hoped I had enough ammo left to finish the job before they finished me. I went into survival mode, a mode that I didn't think I had in me. When your life is on the line you go into autopilot, and your mind either goes into a deep focus or it freezes, and freezing can cause death in split seconds.

We took cover behind a dumpster hoping that we wouldn't get shot in the back. As I ducked behind the dumpster and alley wall, I took a breath and glanced down at my firearm as if I was expecting it to speak to me. My legs were dripping with sweat underneath the heavy layers of Santa gear. They felt like melting popsicles.

My heart was beating as loud as a bass drum. I thought for sure Jasmine could heard it. The Santa boots slid across the broken glass and dirt as I leaned against the dumpster one leg out like a bicycle kick stand. While peeking around the corner, I wondered if we were still being followed or, should I say, hunted.

I saw police cars and lights up ahead in front of St. Andrews Club. *"If we could make it to them and get their attention maybe we can make it out of this with no more gun play,"* I thought.

As I ran towards the police I realized that Jasmine was running in the opposite direction. I yelled for her to get help. Since the car was following me I knew I was the primary target, not Jasmine. I kept thinking, "If I could lure them towards the police, it would be over for them," but, what happened next would be something totally different.

Every step that I took I envisioned that someone in the black car would start shooting and hit me or Jasmine in the back. I could actually taste blood in my mouth. There were moments that I wanted to just turn around and fire multiple shots at the car as it followed us, but something told me not to. I was in survivor mode and that was the only thing on my mind… being a survivor!

Finally, I saw some officers and I thought there was a chance to get help. I ran towards the police screaming "I need help!" The officer turned towards me and said, "Get on the ground now!" pulling out his gun and pointing it at me. Clearly, I was wrong about the police helping me. I quickly dropped down to the ground and put my hands behind my head. All I kept thinking of was the recent police shootings of Black males.

I was terrified to say the least. I could tell right away that they knew something had happened at the gas station. It had to be radioed in to the officers. I could tell they were looking for me. Can you imagine another police shooting in the news? The right headline would have me as the victim, but instead I was perceived as the bad guy. This time it wasn't Mike Brown, Trayvon Martin or Freddie Gray. "In downtown Detroit, an armed Santa Claus shoots two men and is gunned down by police. The Santa was later identified as Marcus Weldon."

"We got him!" they said. Another cop walked over and said "You're one stupid ass! Shooting at a gas station in a Santa suit," as he pinned me down to the ground and handcuffed me. I thought to myself, *"He doesn't even know what happened."* Another police officer appeared out of nowhere yelling, "I seen it all! You're done, buddy." I thought to myself, *"Really? He saw it all, but no one else was even there!"*

As I laid handcuffed on the cold pavement all I could think of was, *"Man, I'm thirsty!"* I felt dehydrated. The adrenaline rush was like an emotional high and I was starting to come down fast. I was surrounded by cops pointing their pistols at me. This is how deer must feel after being hunted and shot down by hunters.

I kept expecting the worst, like the police officer mistakenly discharging his firearm and hitting me in the back while I laid on my belly, leaving my body to bleed out on the street. That would leave the media with the ability to conjure up a story using the picture almost analogous to the Mike Brown photo on the news.

The worst part is hearing the officers celebrate you as their prize while you are still trying to catch your breath and process in your mind on what just happened! Five minutes ago, I was in a shootout. Now, I'm laying here on the ground in handcuffs. "What a turn of events," I muttered.

The police had a whole other plot to this story and I was about to learn the hard way about the necessity of writing your own story before others write it for you. I looked over to my right and saw a man taking a picture of me on the ground. I knew it was only a matter of time before this would go viral, and in only a matter of minutes the news cameras surrounded a tired, skinny, Black Santa.

CHAPTER 3
Welcome to the County

"We're not advocating violence. We're advocates of not being victims."

– James Craig, Detroit Police Chief

In just a few short moments I had gone from having a bright future to not knowing what was going to happen. With pessimistic thoughts looming around me, I felt it would have been better if I was dead than to lose my freedom. As I lay in the back seat of the police car, I asked the police officer if he knew who my Pastor was. I was a productive citizen of Detroit. I was not a criminal! All that meant nothing.

The police officers were treating me like crap, but their own Chief was an advocate for arming yourself. I was just doing what the Police Chief said to do. Nonetheless, in the officer's mind, I was a criminal who fit the stereotype of another "Black, trigger-happy thug". He told me that I better pray that no one was killed because if they were, I would be facing a lot of time. I continued trying to plead my case and quickly remembered to shut my mouth until I could talk to an attorney. This was not the way I was supposed to end my day.

I thought I was going to Wayne County Jail, but

instead, I was taken to the Mound Correctional Facility where I would be held until further notice. It was early in the morning and very dark. It was hard to see, but I could make out tall walls and barbed wire. Inside I was asked to empty my pockets and remove the Santa suit.

Of course, I was the laughing stock of the jail. One layer after another, I stripped and as I took each piece of clothing off, my body started to shake. *"I just shot two guys! Possibly murder and this is a joke to them?"* I thought in anguish, considering what could be my fate.

One of the prison guards was surfing the internet and said, "Congrats! You made the news!" "Wow… For all the wrong reasons!" I replied. I felt powerless to the jokes. I don't think they understood what had just transpired over the last 24 hours. My mind went crazy as I reminded myself of how well my life was going, "I'm a productive citizen! I was just talking to the Mayor last night. I was just excelling in both of my jobs. I'm an entrepreneur! I got a career! What am I doing here?"

The guards continued to joke about me and my situation saying things like, "Well look at Bad Santa!" and "What you getting me for Christmas?" One guard asked me "Why the hell are you dressed as Santa Claus anyway?!" I looked at him like he was he was stupid. "Two can play at this game," I said to myself and then I replied to him, "Well, first off, it's Christmas time and I was being paid $300 to hand out gifts." All the laughter stopped.

One guard inquired, "Damn! Are they hiring?" This told me something pretty obvious. Those guards are not happy with their jobs or their lives. The jokes made them feel better about themselves. I was good at reading people. I mean, I guess it did sound funny.

Here is a skinny guy dressed as Santa Claus and shooting people over Mrs. Claus, but it was serious to me. *"Hell, I know I'm getting paid more than these corny, prison guards!"* I thought to myself.

Breaking my silent thoughts, one guard smirked and said, "Well, looks like your job is about to be doing some hiring," insinuating that I was going to lose my job. Some people join law enforcement to abuse power and to collect a paycheck. Others join to actually protect and serve. But with budget cuts to police officers' pensions, you are not getting the best of the best. You are getting people who join the force as a last result and for the wrong reasons.

I blew off the comments and asked for my phone call. I needed a lawyer and to notify my job that I would not be coming in, but you only get one phone call. This is another problem in this system. They took my cell phone from me for evidence along with my Santa Suit and, since I didn't know any numbers by heart, I could have been hit. As Rick Ector of "Legally Armed in Detroit" put it, "Make the call count!" He's an expert in self-defense who was always on the news.

In a piece Rick wrote on the internet about making your one phone call, he said, "This person should be someone that resides in your local area, someone you trust, and someone who will answer his phone whenever you call. Hopefully, you will have a landline phone number of your designated contact which does not have a collect call block on his telephone. Otherwise, your one phone call from the jail will have been in vain. If your phone call from jail is wasted, you face the worse possible prospect: being incarcerated under tough circumstances over a long weekend with nobody knowing about it."

Luckily, the guard let me use the phone at the desk and I could remember my mom's home number. My mom was actually calm and was already aware of the situation. At the time, I did not know, but there was no time for asking questions.

As a family, we had already been through a lot. We were just worried about my daughter. Mainly because I had just finished a long custody battle and all I could think about was the Court taking her away and giving her back to her mother. Would she understand at the age of five that her dad was in jail for murder? No!

I later found out that a friend of mine who was downtown had called my mother. I had gotten the number for the tow truck from him. The tow truck didn't arrive until well after all of this had gone down. When he arrived, he called my friend and said, "Hey, I'm meeting yo' boy and it looks like a murder scene up here."

My friends jumped in the car and headed to the gas station to see what had happened. They thought I was dead. When they arrived at the gas station and asked the police about me, the police asked, "Who's your friend?" "The guy in the Santa suit," my friends answered. "Oh, he's not dead. He's in custody." So my friend called my mother to let her know I was alive.

I gave my mother the call off number for my job, a

friend who I knew had connections, and a list of contacts that I could remember to call for me. She told me to stay strong and she will contact an attorney for me. It was going to be a long night.

I learned that it takes 72 hours for the court to charge you. If they don't charge you in that amount of time, they must release you. On top of all of this, I was tired and just ready to go to sleep. It was close to 5 o'clock in the morning and my brain was fried. I couldn't wait to get in the bed, but what I had coming was nothing like a bed.

I just couldn't believe all my plans were shattered. It was possible that I wouldn't be spending Christmas with my daughter. My first Christmas after the long custody battle for her was looking like it wasn't going to happen. My idea of being Santa Claus for my baby girl was over. As for me, I could be spending Christmas behind bars.

My Santa suit was in custody as evidence. I transferred to a small holding cell with a toilet and sink. The cell smelled like an alley. There was a lot of graffiti on the walls. There was no bed in the cell, but just the cold, cement floor which would be my bed for the next three days.

I was given cold bologna sandwiches to eat with apple juice. Sometimes they would give me peanut butter sandwiches. The peanut butter and jelly sandwiches were given to you if the guard was feeling generous that day. You might even get an extra apple juice. Yeah, that was a treat! The sandwiches were awful and tasted like cardboard. I would only eat enough not to starve myself out.

Eventually, I used the sandwiches to help pad the floor since I had no mattress or blanket. We had a heater in the cell and I would put the sandwiches on the heater to warm them up and lay on them. So, I used my coat, t-shirt and sandwiches to make a cushion for my back. This was not a joke. It was very real!

There I was, in the prime of my life, experiencing a seemingly endless nightmare. I was filled with embarrassment and shame. "What is everyone going to think of me when they hear this?" I was being haunted by my own thoughts. *"Did I do everything right? Did I pull the trigger at the right time?"* I wondered. Although the shooting was fresh in my mind I couldn't recall everything that happened that night. It was like I was drawing blanks.

I couldn't believe someone was shooting at me. I couldn't believe I shot those guys. "Where did that courage and focus come from?" I asked myself. I don't know what those guys were up to, but whatever it was, it wasn't good and if I didn't react the way I did, Jasmine and I could have been killed.

The same adrenaline I found that night, I needed it in that cell. I wished I could bottle it up and use it whenever I needed it. That survivor mode was unbelievable, but the problem was that it seemed to be gone along with my memory of exactly what happened that night.

It was pretty much a blur of cop lights and gunshots. I felt I was living in someone's movie. This doesn't happen to people normally. I mean, my life as a whole, that is. This was just the tipping point of the unpredictability and craziness of my life story. No matter how good life was going for me, the devil seemed to have something up his sleeve every single time!

As I began to doze off on the sandwich bags, I found myself having flashback nightmares of those cold, hard steel handcuffs and the feeling of the cold pavement pushing against my face as I lay on the ground. I could feel the cops with their guns drawn on me all around me in the cell. The nightmares were so real and scary.

At times, I believed someone was in my cell talking to me. I thought I was going crazy! But the voices were actually the police officers and guards ushering in more criminals into the larger cell across from me. It must have been a busy night that night because it felt like everyone was inside of there.

The cell I was in was in a basement and had a small window at the top of it. There was no clock in sight. I could see the grass and the reflection of the sun off of the grass. I had to do what they did in ancient times and look at the sunset to tell the time. In other cells, there was no window. Prisoners would go for days without sunlight.

People are dehumanized in a holding cell. You have given up your right to be treated like a human once you are accused of committing a crime. The key word is "accused." The things you take for granted everyday like brushing your teeth, taking a shower and using normal bathroom amenities are gone for at least 72 hours.

If you are lucky, you may get a guard to give you toilet paper, but most likely that stuff is not supplied until you are transferred over to Wayne County Jail after either you are charged and can't post bail or don't get a bond.

Sometimes, I had to do some degrading things like use the sandwich bags to wipe myself after using the disgusting toilet.

There were other inmates there in orange jumpsuits. You can tell that they been there for some time. They were mopping floors and they were actually the one's passing out the sandwiches for us to eat. One of the guards chuckled, laughing at me, and told one of the inmates in an orange jumpsuit that I was the Santa shooter. The inmate looked at me in shock and shouted, "Him?!" He couldn't believe it.

I was the talk of the correctional facility. Everybody wanted to see me. They wanted to see who this guy was that shot people downtown while wearing a Santa suit. Although when the inmate looked at me, I didn't quite fit their idea of a Santa or a shooter. I guess he was expecting a bigger, rougher looking guy. I suppose I didn't look like I would do something like that. To me, that was a good thing.

The guards were assholes and, as I stated earlier, they loved to joke about my case. Usually the guards are want-to-be cops that aren't used to having any authority. Like all people, they have problems at home that they bring to work, but just imagine someone bringing their problems to work in an uncontrolled and unsupervised place.

Jail is a place where guards have to watch "accused" criminals and if the guard decides to treat you like 3/5 human, there is no Human Resources or Union to complain to. Even if you do complain, your image and word is now tainted. In other words, no one would believe your story. The best thing you can do is wait, but waiting can feel like the hardest thing to do.

At first, I was quarantined. I was alone and I thought that was best. I paced back and forth. Eventually, though, I started talking to other people. Humans are social creatures and being alone is not something we really like.

I started asking questions like, "Hey, man, what time is it? What happens next? Do you know? How long can they keep me in here? I need to take a shower." "Man, you got a while before that," one of the other prisoners said emphatically. You realize how much you really need people – especially when you don't know what's going on.

The next day, a guard came over to my cell. "You have a visitor," he said. I was brought into a small room with a glass and table dividing the room. On the other side, a middle-aged white man name Dennis walked in. He was really thin and wore a brown suit. He had curly, white hair and looked like an old, University professor. He was the attorney that my parents hired.

We had to use these old landline phones to speak to each other. He asked me what happened the night before, but I could barely hear him. The phones were raggedy, just like the toilet and everything else in that place.

I gave him a brief rundown of what happened. He then told me not make any statements to the detectives. He kept pounding that into my head. He told me that it's going to be hard sitting in there fearing the unknown.

He assured me that he was good at what he does and to "let him work." I had to trust him a little, but my real trust was in God and I was praying that He would bring me through this.

As the guard walked me back to my cell, he said something that I would never forget: "Your problem is that you shot two Arabs, and they stick together. You'll be lucky to get your mom and dad to come to court with you. You know we don't stick together." "So, they were Arabs," I whispered, confirming my own suspicion. Back in my cell, I waited another fifty-two hours before I would hear something.

My thoughts started to spin again and I began contemplating a lot of questions. All I could think about was, "Why? Why would they start something with us? What was their plan? If the situation was on the opposite shoe, how would they feel?" Think about it. If I hopped out of a car at a gas station and started pushing on an Arabian woman and the Arabian male who was with her saw it, oh boy, talk about a problem!

That guy probably would have killed me and anyone with me. They do not play when it comes to their women and they shouldn't. Women are to be respected and it's disrespectful to put your hands on them regardless of their race. But why wasn't the same respect given to African-American women? Are they not on the same level as Arabian women?

I was reminded of a story an Arabian co-worker told me a while ago. There was a famous Arabian pornography star named Mia Khalifa who disgraced her family's name by doing porn. Pornography is understandably disgraceful, but what stood out to me the most in this conversation we had was when he said, "Oh yeah, and when she did a porn video with those Black guys, I bet her family was really upset!" "But why would race matter?" I wondered. Porn is porn, but I started to understand that the respect for Blacks amongst other races was very low.

I don't like to pull the race card, but think about it. It's like we are at the bottom of the food chain. It feels like no one has respect for the Black man or woman. We aren't taken seriously on anything. Our image has always been tainted through mass media and we, as Black people, have given them the ammunition to use against us. The other ethnic groups stick together. The prison guard was right… maybe.

I was determined to make sure that my mom and dad were not the only ones in the courtroom. "I can't let the system railroad me," I determined. I could only hope, as I laid in that cell, that my lawyer was finding evidence to prove my innocence. I was already viewed as a criminal, according to the police, and I knew that I was about to get a full dose of how it feels to be in the justice system.

My daydreaming was soon over when a police officer came to my cell and told me it was time for my video arraignment. A video arraignment is a live, formal reading of a criminal charging document in the presence of the defendant to inform the defendant of the charges against him. In response to the arraignment, the accused is expected to enter a plea.

Acceptable pleas vary, but they generally include "guilty" and "not guilty". All of this is done through a television monitor. So while you're in jail, the court has you on a screen to read your charges to you with your lawyer present (if you have one). This was the first time I heard what I was being charged with.

The judge looked at me and read off a long list of charges. "Count 1 and 2 both assault with intent to murder, punishable by life or any number of years. Count 3 and 4 assault with intent to do great bodily harm less than murder punishable by maximum of ten years. Counts 5 and 6 are assault with a dangerous weapon punishable by maximum of 4 years. And count 7, weapons felony firearm, mandatory 2 years consecutively with preceding any term of imprisonment imposed for the felony or attempted felony conviction."

After the charges were read, I stood there in my bright red North Face® jacket and brown jeans stunned. My head slightly tilted to the left like a confused dog. I was looking into the screen in disbelief, hoping that the guards and inmates couldn't see the emotions bleeding out of my pores. The fact of the matter was that seven felonies could easily mean life in prison and I wasn't ready to hear that.

My legs got weak and I felt sick, but that wasn't the worst of it. My video arraignment would be broadcasted on all the local Detroit news stations. My business would soon be everyone's business, and with public announcement comes public opinion.

My attorney submitted a plea of "not guilty" to all seven counts. It turned out that the police department was having trouble finding me in the computer as a concealed weapon license holder. My attorney told them that was a mistake and that I have a CPL permit. This put into perspective how unorganized the Detroit justice system really is.

I had my permit for six years and even had to renew it. I mulled over all of this in my mind, thinking, *"How much more of this can I take? These three days were hell already and now these trumped up charges, along with being unorganized spell disaster for sure."*

My bail was set at $50,000 and I had to pay ten percent, which was $5,000 to get out of jail. I'll explain later what happens when you can't pay. Afterwards, I was chained by the ankles together with eight other inmates and our hands were cuffed behind our backs. We resembled the chain gangs, like you see on television. The other inmates were wearing jeans, Timberlands, and t-shirts. We were put in the back of a police van to be transferred to Wayne County where I would have to wait to be bailed out.

The police van was hot and dark. Every time they would hit a corner, we were sliding back and forth. It felt like there were no shocks on the van. We were still chained together and sitting on benches without seatbelts. I was crammed between the wall and a big dude that smelled like a wet dog. Of course, he hadn't showered in four days either. I probably smelled like him and couldn't tell. But the funk of the un-showered inmates was the least of my worries. We were headed to another nightmare… the County!

In Wayne County, it was a different sight. I saw women in prison jumpsuits along with men, but all separated. All I heard was loud yelling, cursing and young kids rapping lyrics to their favorite songs out loud. Men were talking to women saying, "Hey baby!" They knew it would be a while before they saw women again. Roaches navigated across the cold floor looking for food. As big as they were, it was obvious they were eating quite well. Clearly, they were being fed and treated better than the inmates!

Wayne County sheriffs were everywhere and they had attitudes. They had a tough job dealing with the rowdy crowd. In their minds, if you were here, you must have done something wrong, which means you do not deserve respect. They would talk to us like we were dirt or worst. You might ask them a serious question and they would talk to you poorly or completely ignore you.

I'm very observant of people. Some of these guards want to serve and protect and some have a chip on their shoulders. Some really wanted to be police officers but didn't for whatever reason. Those types tend to over-exert their power or authority.

There was a light-skinned prison guard, who was about 5'4" and wore thick glasses. He looked like a Smurf and he was really mean. He was super aggressive for seemingly no reason. He couldn't talk normally. He was always yelling. I was curious as to what made him act like this. Perhaps the other guards treated him badly and he took it out on us. You had to know which guard to talk to because some really treated you wrong.

I was put into a big cell with the rest of the people from the other jail on Mound Road. After getting settled in the cell full of other inmates waiting to be processed to the County, I began to scope out the area. Rusted toilets, cracked paint, foul smells and graffiti was obviously the norm when it comes down to jail. It's all you experience everywhere you turn.

The cell I was in had one toilet and a sink. As I talked to one guy who was next to me about the prosecutors and how they operate, I could see how we were all considered just numbers being processed through a system. Some guys seemed to enjoy it as it validated them in the street life.

Overhearing my conversation, a young guy asked me, "Ah, you the nigga in the Santa suit?" He was laughing. He was a young, skinny kid wearing a sweat jump suit that looked like it was about 15 years old. I didn't respond right away because I was trying to figure out his angle.

He quickly followed up by saying, "Bro, I seen it on *Crime in the D*." *Crime in the D* was a popular social media site that kept Detroit updated on crimes in the city. Apparently, my case was a hot topic and, obviously, this guy pointed me out from the picture he saw. "You shot 2 niggas! That shit crazy!" he said, sounding like he was respecting the fact that I shot somebody.

A lot of people in jail think it's a cool, gangster thing to shoot someone. I felt it was unfortunate. I had too much going on to have something like this happen to me. I wanted to explain to them that I wasn't a killer, but "don't push me" like Tupac said. In the same breath, at that moment, I would've taken it all back. I probably wouldn't have even helped the girl with the tire. Honestly, I wasn't thinking. Clearly, it wasn't my fault or hers. Second guessing if you did everything right was probably the norm in situations like this.

There was a nurse in the jail who asked us if we had any medical conditions and fingerprinted us. We were officially a part of the system. Some of us became property of the State of Michigan.

Everyone who committed a felony had on a red band and everyone who committed a misdemeanor was given a blue band. Of course, I had a red one, but what hurt the most was seeing so many young kids under the age of twenty-one in there. Kids being there for drug offenses and carjacking was very common. The worst part was that the majority were Black males. This was not what I wanted to see.

I was trying to figure out why people did what they did without being too nosey. There was one guy who was very quiet. He was a big Mexican guy. He had a jumpsuit on from another county, maybe from another state. You could tell he had done some time before.

Someone saw that I had my attorney's card in my hand and asked me who he was. I said, "Dennis Craig." The Mexican guy overheard me talking about my attorney. He sat up and said, "You got who? Dennis?" I repeated my attorney's name. "Oh, yeah, he's good" he said,

"He beat my first murder case." "What did you do now?" I asked. "You don't want to know," he said and he laid back down. For a moment, I had a little comfort.

A lot of kids were in there for stupid stuff. One 17-year-old boy told me that he was in jail for carjacking. When I asked him why he did it, he said, "Man, I don't know. I was just bored." I found out that a lot of people just wanted some type of thrill in their lives. When you are deprived of opportunity and you feel like there's nothing worth living for, you need some type of excitement. If you're not goal-oriented, and you don't know what you want to do in life, you'll just do stuff like you're on auto-pilot.

I wanted to reach out and tell those young guys, "Don't have an idle mind, dude. Pick a goal and stick with it! Learn how to think about the long term and not just short term. Stop hanging around negative thinkers!" I know everyone wants to have friends, but you can find friends who have the same goals as you. Like the old saying goes, "birds of a feather flock together."

If you're trying to be a doctor, you'll need friends in medical school. If you want to be a lawyer, hang out with people in law school. Entrepreneurs hang out with entrepreneurs. Thugs hang out with thugs. Drug dealers hang out with drug dealers. You will be just like those with whom you spend your time.

That 17-year-old boy had a son who was just a couple of months old. There were so many Black men in there who kept saying things like, "Oh man, I'm going to miss my son!" The jail was full of men who seemed like they wanted to be fathers. You could see where all of the fathers are going. If they don't come out, there will be many fatherless children. I began to think about my daughter while I was in there and the little comfort I had was gone.

The most degrading thing I saw was grown men being stripped naked and forced to open up their butts and cough. They had to open their mouths and stick out their tongues to ensure they hadn't brought any drugs into the jail. The smell of unwashed ass swept the room, making my eyes water, and even gag. I turned my head away and looked at the television screen in the policeman's office ahead of me and there was my face on the news.

The news story was about me, the "Santa Shooter", with a mug shot of me ten years ago. Then, it hit me like a ton of bricks. *"Kill me now!"* I hollered in my mind. Everything around me seemed to go on pause and, even though I couldn't hear the volume on the television, it seemed to drown out all of the noise around me.

On the television screen, there was a picture of me when I was 17-years-old. I had suppressed a memory of that day in my subconscious all of this time. All of a sudden, I remembered these walls and the smell of this building. The County was familiar to me. I wasn't always innocent. I had a past and its picture had come to haunt me.

CHAPTER 4
Never Ride 4-Deep

"We have all done something dreadful in our lives, or have felt the urge to."

– *Wilma Derksen, David and Goliath: Underdogs, Misfits, and The Art of Battling Giants by Malcolm Gladwell*

One night, three friends and I drove to a friend's house on 8 mile and Kelly. It was the first time we had ever been to her house, so we did not know the exact location. It was so dark that we really could not see the addresses on the houses. After circling the block twice trying to find it, we were pulled over by two, white police officers.

After asking me for my license and registration, one officer said that I was acting suspicious driving around the block. "I was looking for my friend's house. I couldn't see the addresses on the house and wasn't sure if I was on the right block," I tried to explain. He told me to get out of the car. Even though I was afraid, I got out of the vehicle.

I put my hands behind my back and was handcuffed. The officer put me in the backseat of the police car and he and the other officer began to search my car. Then, they put everyone else in handcuffs on the ground.

After about thirty minutes of searching, they let us go and told us to get to our destination. Disgusted and humiliated, I took everyone home and we never went to our friend's house. I told her later that night what happened and said, "Next time, turn a porch light on. You know we can't be riding around 4-deep around Eight Mile looking for an address! We looked suspicious!"

I know some things now that I didn't know then. I know one thing for sure: Never ride four-deep late at night in Detroit. Four Black kids in a car get profiled as thugs in an urban city. It doesn't matter what you're doing. It doesn't matter where you're going.

Looking back on the situation, I shouldn't have made a statement. The officer wasn't supposed to search my car. He had no reason to pull me over, let alone ask me to get out of my car and search me, but I didn't know any better. None of my friends knew any better either. Fortunately, they didn't fully search my car. We would have had a completely different outcome that night.

When I was a teenager, the peer pressure to be considered a thug was real. When we come into our own as young Black males, we don't want to be outcasts. We want to fit in – with somebody, anybody! I mean, think about this: Everything you see on TV points to the thug life. Every time Blacks get acknowledged for a good role in a movie, it's for the bad things they do. It's either a thug role or a woman in a compromising position, some kind of sex position or sex type of role. Think about it!

Do you remember Denzel Washington in Training Day or Halle Berry in Monster's Ball? That image is out there and that is what is promoted and even celebrated. Those images are who we're pushed to look up to and become. In your mind, subconsciously, you think, *"Okay, it's not cool to be smart. It's not cool to keep your pants pulled up. What's cool is selling drugs, having sex, robbing people and stealing stuff."*

That's what makes you feel like you're something. I reached a point where I gave up on finding hope in anything different. I kept thinking that and related thoughts like, "I'm not going to school. These schools they give us aren't up to par anyway. The books are outdated. I don't have no pride in this!"

When I was in middle school, I was curious about the world around me. I would build robots from old motors and household items. I built model cars. I would ask questions about things that other kids wouldn't normally ask like, "Who gave the colors their names?" It may sound funny, but what I was doing at a young age was trying to connect the dots. Still, I let my surrounding environment destroy my curiosity by trying to fit in with my peers.

The neighborhood schools in Detroit all had nicknames. Murphy Wright was nicknamed "Murder Wright." Finney was nicknamed "The Pen", which referred to the nickname for penitentiaries, or prisons. The schools that were named after African-American leaders like Frederick Douglas, Marcus Garvey and Martin Luther King, Jr. were actually a contradiction to what those leaders stood for. Most of the schools were in poverty-stricken areas which negatively and psychologically impacts the image of these leaders in the minds of the children.

It's just bad and I knew it first-hand because I had experiences both in the Detroit Public School system and in suburban school districts. Believe me when I tell you, it's different! Even now, as an adult, I see that DPS still hasn't cleaned up its act.

On a clip from "The Young Turks" on YouTube, they reported on the current Detroit Mayor, Mike Duggan's, tour of the schools in response to teachers' "Sick-Out" protest. They said the mayor "...saw kids with coats on in the classroom as well as a dead mouse lying in a trap right out in the open, and he called what he witnessed throughout his DPS tour 'deeply disturbing'."

I've seen both sides of the fence. I can see how you get caught up in what's going on. In high school, I got caught up, too. I mean, I wasn't always like I am now. I actually had my gangster days back then and I know exactly why I did it. I was just trying to fit in.

In high school, it's like, you only have a few choices. If you're smart, you sit with the geniuses. They are the "nerds", right? Then, you have the sports jocks who play sports like football and basketball. You have a promising type of career possibly so you just hang with them. Then, you get the "populars". This group includes the "Ladies' Men" and the guy who's into whatever girls like fashion-wise.

Finally, you have the last group, the odd balls, who don't fit into any other group. If you're in this group, your parents don't have the money to buy you the expensive gym shoes. You get laughed at a lot. So, you end up trying to be harder than everybody – the nerds, the sports jocks, and the populars. You say, "Okay, you know how I'm gonna get attention? I'm gonna bully or act like I'm gonna be hard. Then, I'll stand out. Then, I'll be somebody!" That's what it is.

At first, I was kind of neutral because I wasn't a straight-A student, although I was smart. I wasn't a nerd. I wasn't a jock. I was short in high school, so I couldn't really get into sports. As far as fashion, my mom bought me conservative clothes because she knew I could get robbed easily. That left me without a group. I had to find something or somebody to clique with. So, I ended up falling into that Odd Ball trap.

I was looking for people to have my back and feel like I had a family at school. I don't know why I felt that way now, but as a kid in high school you feel like you have to be with somebody. You can't be an outcast. You can't be sitting somewhere in the corner by yourself. You need somebody. It's like jail because people do the same thing there. They clique up with their folks, too. While I was trying to survive in Detroit Public High Schools, I had to find my group.

This was especially important after school was out. Then, other high school students come to your school and try to start stuff with you. Detroit are literally like gangs.

Back in the day, it was like Finney vs. Murphy Wright or Finney vs. Osborne. When they came to our school with their groups and asked, "You go to Finney?" BOOM! They'd smash you! Suburban schools don't have to deal with that. They can focus on what you're supposed to at school, like academics.

There was also a light-skinned vs. dark-skinned beef in school. The light-skinned guys always felt they had to prove themselves to the dark-skinned guys that tried to punk them. A friend of mine was light-skinned and he got into a fight with a guy just because of his complexion. The dark-skinned guy decided he was going to mess up the face of my friend. He put a lock in his hand and started a fight. My friend's face was trashed!

It's worse if you have something nice when you're at school. That can go wrong any minute. I lived in the neighborhood of 6 Mile and Gunston. That wasn't the greatest area. Later, I moved to East Warren and Cadieux and that area was cool, but you still had people just being ruthless and acting like they didn't have home training. If you had anything nice, they were just going to take it. It kinda forced you to be hard.

"You got nice Jordan's on." You almost don't want to hear that. When I was catching the bus, I put my Jordan's in my book bag and put my raggedy shoes on because I knew if I didn't change shoes, I would get robbed!

One day, I had a red and white Sean John outfit on with red and white Jordan's. This outfit was like a couple of hundred dollars. I thought someone would eventually catch on to me hiding my shoes in my book bag so I started taking my clothes off in the locker room before getting on the bus. I remember that my boy got robbed at a bus stop and he was bare footed in the snow! I didn't want that to happen to me.

After the 9th or 10th grade, I started getting rides to and from school and no longer riding the bus because of this. You know your environment. You either get out of it or you become a part of it in ways you never thought you would. The bottom line is, as long as you're there, you have to learn how to survive in it.

One way for me to survive in my mind was to start working. My father instilled a strong work ethic in me and, when I was in the 8th grade, I started working at the bookstore at my school. We were just organizing shelves, going outside and cleaning up around the school and stuff like that. It was just odd jobs, but it taught me to work. Your work ethic is your calling card. Hard work pays off.

By the time I was seventeen, I was working part-time at Farmer Jack Supermarket and I was cutting grass. I was finally able to get my own car. It was a '95 burgundy Grand Marquis. Imagine an old police car without the lights and stuff. I had the loud booming speaker system, a little chrome and 20's (rims). I was happy until my car was broken into and I thought I might get robbed.

I thought this was the work of a guy I used to get into it with at school. He would often pull his knife out to threaten me and other people. I thought, *"If he's got a knife, I'll get something better."*

All I knew at that point was that I did not want to tell my father. You can't do that because then you come across like a cry baby. My dad knew that somebody broke into my car, but I told him, "It was probably just a crackhead or something." You see, I was going to Cass Tech at the time, so I knew he would believe me. Cass Corridor was a really bad part of town!

I would see people drinking 40-ounces of beer and prostitutes on the street. It was all kinds of stuff going on at the time down there, so, I just blamed it on them. But, I knew deep inside that I had a problem that needed to be addressed because there were some kids that were trying me. They were faking like they were my friends, but they were secretly watching me. I thought they were all my friends, but one, in particular, completely tricked me.

It was easy to trick me because I was really kind-hearted. I was naïve and I didn't know the street rules. So, I found out that every time I turned around, some kids were talking about me with other people.

They saw me get nice, new things. I was getting jewelry, those nice outfits and the newest shoes. I got my nice car and the girls' attention started to come my way. I was finding my little spot. In high school, with no bills and earning like $200 dollars a week, I was set!

Few people had cars in 12th grade. Dudes would get in my car and say, "Let's go to the store," or "Oh, he has a screen radio," or "Oh, he got sounds!" Sure, some people had cars, but not with all that. Later, I found out they were secretly telling folks, "Yo, break in his car." They took advantage of me because I was being so nice.

I decided I wasn't going to let that happen again. I was thinking, "They ain't gone get me this time! I'mma have protection." My girlfriend's brother at the time was "the Hood Dude" and he sold guns. He talked me into it, too, saying, "You know you need to get you a gun. You can't just be letting them take yo' stuff. 'Cause a lot of people have the butterfly knives. They will pull a butterfly knife in a minute and what you gone do? You just gone let them punk you? What you gone do?" He just wanted to make a sale, but I bought a gun from him anyway.

I had to change my image a little bit. I started to build a persona when I got my gun. I was not born a hard, gangsta. However, I was able to blend in. I made sure my pants were sagging. I wore my hat backwards or to the side. I smoked a Black & Mild from time to time. I would try to dumb down my speech and talk as ignorantly as possible. I would play the raunchiest music. I would only secretly listen to Michael Jackson. I loved the Jackson 5! Who didn't?

I finally had him. My first gun was an old, rusted .38 caliber. I will never forget it. I called him "Dirty Harry." I paid $125 dollars for him. Dirty Harry was all black with a brown, wooden handle that was chipped. He was old like the old Western, revolver handguns with a spinning barrel. It came with a box of 30 bullets. I held him up in the air and pulled his rusted trigger. A bullet went flying up into the atmosphere. He worked! That's all I needed to know.

I took Dirty Harry to school with me every day. I left him in the car, but sometimes I would bring him with me because I was afraid somebody would break into the car and take him. I never got caught with him in school because the metal detectors never worked. I was ready to handle things myself. I was ready to be a man. At least, that's what I told myself. The truth is, I was very afraid.

I thought about the guy who probably broke into my car. I remember him vividly. They used to call him

"Killa" because he carried a knife and a gun. This was the guy I would get into it with from time to time. He was the reason I got Dirty Harry.

I wasn't going to let Killa, or anybody else, pull their knives or guns on me. I wasn't even thinking about what would happen if I used Dirty Harry. Let me tell you – it's the things that happen when you're not thinking that you will regret for your entire life!

I bought the gun because I was scared. There was a lot going on, but Killa was my biggest challenge at the moment. I knew Killa kept all types of weapons, but one day, some news slipped out about this so called "Killa" through a female friend of mine. "He acts so tough, but he leaves his gun in the car under the seat because he's scared to bring it in," she revealed. The girl was obviously upset with him for something and now she was doing what we called "dry snitching". (This was basically indirectly telling on someone.)

I took this new information and acted on it. I skipped class and, along with a neighborhood friend, worked out the plan to get into Killa's car and take the gun. To get into his car, we had to be discreet. Black hoodies and a pump airsoft pellet gun was all we needed.

The pellet gun was used to freeze and shatter the glass window. Once the pellet was fired, it would hit the glass window and, if done correctly, it would freeze it. Then, we could literally just touch the glass and seconds later it would shatter. It would break without the explosive, shattering noises that a hammer or a brick would produce. The plan was solid and it worked like a charm!

Once we broke the glass, we went through the vehicle like mice going through the pantry. We took everything we could find. We took CDs, the radio and, of course, the black pistol that made him a "killa." I felt it would even up the playing field. "Now, let's see how tough he really is without it," I plotted. He wasn't so tough without his gun after all. He took off running down the street, knowing that I had the upper-hand. I felt like I had conquered a big obstacle in my life at that moment.

After the word got around of Killa's reaction that day, that tough guy stuff went out the window. But then, I was beginning to change and being pulled into a lifestyle that wasn't me. My grades soon dropped and school was no longer as important to me as being tough.

The new gangster mentality was growing in me. I fell victim to the subconscious onslaught of the gangster movies, music and my environment. I tried my best to imitate them because the image kept me safe from wolves and accepted by my peers.

My mom took me out of Cass and put me into Avondale High School in Auburn Hills. Soon, I saw opportunities. I saw the best of both worlds. By me being in the suburbs half of the time and in the hood the other half, I started selling drugs to the suburb kids. They were scared to go into Detroit to get them but, of course, I was from Detroit. The same guy I bought my gun from also had a lot of weed. The kids in the suburbs would pay top dollar for a little bag. I would go back and forth making transactions, not thinking of repercussions.

The hood dudes in the neighborhood off Nottingham and 3 Mile on the eastside loved when I would show up to "re-up" because it meant money. You see, I didn't have to "hustle" to survive, but they did. I did this for extra money and because I thought it was cool.

My mother and father both worked and I had a job at 16. Eventually, those same guys tried to rob me while I was chillin' with my people in front of my house. These dudes pulled up on us with masks and hopped out of their car trying to rob us. One had a black pistol. I could sense something wasn't right when I saw this car pulling up on us slowly. I left my gun in the car so I was naked.

My adrenaline was already pumping. As soon as they stepped out of the car and I saw that gun, I turned around and ran. I heard footsteps behind me like the guy was hot on my trail. The hairs stood up on my back like a porcupine. Turns out it was my friend, "White Boi", running alongside of me! As my heart pumped, I leaped over my backyard fence, in a single bound, and landed face first into the mud. I just knew I was going to get shot in the back, but I didn't.

The young hoodlums didn't even chase us. Once we ran, they jumped back into the car. They left us with muddy outfits and broken pride. Later, I found out it was the guys who sold me the illegal merchandise. They were secretly scheming on how to get me because they were full of jealousy.

Two months after that, one of the guys was killed in a robbery gone bad. Needless to say, I dodged that bullet and stopped selling weed. But I couldn't stop carrying my gun. Eventually, it would cost me. Although Cass

Tech was not a bad school academically, it still fell victim to the detrimental and harsh circumstances of the surrounding Detroit area. My neighborhood school was ten times worse than Cass. So my mom did everything she could to keep me out of the neighborhood school and that environment.

In order for me to change school districts, my mom had to give legal guardianship of me to my Aunt Tina who lived in the Auburn Hills area. I moved in with my aunt and was accepted into the school. However, this new gangsta mentality was now embedded in me. I kept my gun with me still and would soon pay for it.

Unfortunately, being a young Black male with the type of car I had, I used to get pulled over a lot. The police would harass me all the time. They would pull me over and stretch me out for no reason. They would say things like, "Oh, you didn't have your turn signal on. Get out the car!" I would take Dirty Harry out of the car often because I was scared that they would find it. I used to hide it in the trunk or in the engine, but one day, I had Dirty Harry in the car while I was riding with some friends.

I was driving on the west side of Detroit with my brother and some friends. The police saw us and turned on their lights like it was December 1st Christmas tree lighting time. First, they asked me how old I was. Then, I told them how old my brother was and I thought, *"Shoot, he's a minor!"* Immediately the officer said, "Get out the car. We gone take him to jail. He shouldn't be out this late."

It was midnight, beyond the city curfew, which was 10 p.m. They patted me down and found Dirty Harry.

Dang! We were thrown in the back of the police car. I remember one officer throwing my Carhartt jacket over my head, covering my face as I sat in the back. They took us all in. I kept praying that the cops wouldn't take us somewhere and beat our asses. I liked my face!

The police took photos of us that night. I remember that I had about ten to twelve cornrow braids in my hair. I was wearing a Miami Heat jersey with black Sean John jeans and some black, white and gold Jordans. This is the photo I saw when I was sitting at Wayne County. That photo was not supposed to show up again.

I took advantage of the Holmes Youthful Trainee Act (HYTA) program that was supposed to expunge my record after a certain time period, including photos. Attorney Loren Dickstein wrote an online article posted on October 9, 2011 stating, "The program helps young people keep a youthful mistake off their record, so they don't have to worry about one lapse of judgment ruining their future. Essentially, a youthful offender has the opportunity to get a second chance."

"Stupid HYTA program!" I scoffed, while I was sitting at the County, looking at the picture on the T.V. After 10 years, that picture was supposed to go away, but that didn't happen for the "Shooting Santa". I dropped to the floor and leaned against the wall next to the stinking urinal. "Wow," I thought. "My past has come back to haunt me." Just when it seems you take five steps forward, life takes you ten steps backward.

CHAPTER 5
Media Blitz

"The media's the most powerful entity on earth. They have the power to make the innocent guilty and to make the guilty innocent, and that's power. Because they control the minds of the masses."

- Malcolm X

"Weldon! Your bail has been placed. Step up!" A police officer yelled to me, but I was frozen stuck on the television. My 17-year-old face was posted on the news and I was Public Enemy Number 1. Detroit's "Shooting Santa" was a great Christmas story for the viewers and I knew they were eating it up all over the city.

The loud, gruff voice of the officer quickly snapped me out of it. "Boy, get the hell up before you end up staying another night!" I got up immediately and followed the officer. As I walked out, the Mexican inmate said, "You're a good kid. You don't belong here. Don't come back here again. Don't waste your life." From the brief moments we spoke, he could tell that I wasn't a killer. He himself was a killer and he told me earlier that he was going to be spending the rest of his life in prison. I stopped and nodded my head and responded, "I won't."

He was right. I didn't belong there, but there I was

walking away from him to the next thing I was unsure of. *"I'm not a criminal, but the news says I am,"* I thought, as I walked out of the cell. It's not what you say, it's what you can prove in this world and I'm going to have to do a lot of proving.

Black, legal gun owners are often victims of unconscious biases, stereotypes and looked at as scapegoats for crime. Whether it's an Aeropostale®, Guess®, or a True Religion® brand hoodie, it's the same look being perpetrated through advertisement for both black and white teens. It's the hot style for young kids and it got Trayvon Martin stereotyped, stalked, and killed. But, would that same urban clothing look on a young white boy get him stalked by "you-know-who"?

Today, in America, it is really easy to demonize the legal gun owners and bunch them in the same classification as illegal gun owners. Pacifist politicians and prosecutors are extremely hard on gun owners and are enforcing stiffer penalties on gun crimes. A Black man with a gun is automatically stereotype as an illegal carrier or a hot-headed thug with a gun. This was the stereotype I was up against at first glance.

At home, I was greeted by my family and pastor who all wanted to know if I was unharmed. I told them I was okay and just needed a long shower and a whole pizza to myself. I was smelly and hungry, like a homeless man on the street.

My back was sore from lying on the hard floor for three days. My mind raced from one extreme to another as I thought about my job and my daughter. "What was my job thinking? Would they fire me? But they know me! They know my character. Or do they?" I contemplated these things within myself as we headed home.

As I walked into the house, my daughter ran and jumped in my arms. I know she had to smell my body odor, but she didn't care. Daddy was home. She had not seen me for almost four days. She could sense the tension in the air. Something was wrong with her father. She could pick up on the fact that things weren't right by the tone of my voice and my mother's reaction. I tried to hold back the tears, but I couldn't any longer. I cried and told her I missed her. The hug and the smile from her made me realize that, in the blink of an eye, I could be lost in the justice system and my child would go fatherless.

My girlfriend was there, too. I hugged her and gave her a kiss on the cheek. She held me tight and told me she was there for me. She was probably thinking, "Look at this nigga'! Hanging out all night with homegirl, going to two parties and then ended up in jail! Who does that?" She kept her thoughts to herself during that moment, but I knew I was going to hear it later.

I had to snap out of it. There was work to be done. I quickly called my job to call off work for the next day. I was hoping that they wouldn't try to jump the gun and fire me because of this. I wanted them to give me a chance to claim my innocence.

My boss answered and told me that he would put me down for a sick day. He also told me that I was good on his end, but Human Resources wanted to call me. Basically, it was out of his hands and up to them on my future at the casino. HR wanted to meet with me before I could come back to work. It was more like "if" I could come back to work.

"If I lose my job, how will I pay for a lawyer? Are they judging me already?" I wondered about the answers to those questions after I got off the phone with my manager. Then, I thought about my job at the liquor promotion company. Maybe I could work with them and go out on a stress leave at the casino until things die down a little with the media attention on the case. I called my manager at the liquor company who explained to me as much as they would love for me to come back, I couldn't come back until the case was resolved. (Unlike the casino, I wasn't in a union, so they could just fire me at will.)

Next thing I knew, I was even removed from the Mayor's Recreation Board. I was too hot! Those things I worked hard for were slowly being taken from me. My chivalrous act had turned into a calamity. I was no longer the Fox 2 model or Pastor Bell's mentee. I was the "Santa Shooter" on every news station.

My phone rang nonstop. My phone and Facebook page were blowing up with messages from people who wanted to help me and some who were just plain nosey. I had people contact me that I haven't spoken with in years! My business was everyone's business. I quickly learned that not everyone who calls has your best interest at heart.

"The HYTA program lied to me!" I muttered. "They said this would never be brought up again." In this picture, I fit America's black thug stereotype: young, Black dude with cornrow braids. This picture incriminates me before I can even get a fair trial. It seemed to set the tone of this whole case. This is why your reputation in life means everything. They created a villain on Christmas, "Bad Santa," with this picture and this contrived story.

I felt sick as hell. No words can describe the feeling in my stomach. Even the Detroit Police Chief, James Craig, made jokes about my case on Fox 2, saying things like "Santa was packing more than just presents."

My uncle called from Philadelphia. I made the New York Times! The Santa Shooter of Detroit was apparently big holiday news. You can imagine how shocked my family was in Philly hearing that their nephew was involved in a shooting incident and he wasn't "the victim."

Chief Craig also bragged about how good the police work was in catching the "Santa Shooter." If the police work was so good, why didn't they find the Arabian man's gun? And wasn't this the same man advocating for protecting yourself? The Chief was a strong advocate of citizens not being victims and being armed to protect themselves.

Chief Craig was on the cover of the NRA magazine for these comments. But, now with this mendacious story the media has put out, he is speaking out against a clean-cut civilian. A single father with a full-time job. "Are Black people not allowed to defend themselves? Get your facts straight, Mr. Chief Craig!" I yelled at the television.

My mom was doing everything she could to help

me. She called the police station demanding to talk to the sergeant in charge of my case. When she got him on the phone, she asked if there was any video tape of the incident and if so what was on it. The sergeant in charge of my case told her that "the tape won't help or hurt him." Now what on earth could that mean? Sounded like more conspiracy to me.

I couldn't help but to read the comments about me on different articles online. "Hang the Nigger," one man wrote under one photo of me. Some people even went back and forth with my friends who tried to defend me with positive comments. How can people be so judgmental?

I even had a mentor who was a V.I.P. in the city that wouldn't even return my calls, emails or texts because she was afraid that it would taint her image. She could no longer be associated with me. No one wants to be labeled a mentor or friend of a shooting Santa Claus. I learned a very hard lesson with this.

People will turn their backs on you to protect their own reputation. No one, and no company, wants to be involved with a criminal. It's bad for business. Both the liquor company and the casino's names were all over the news.

The red carpet was pulled from under me. It was just like what happens to the NBA and NFL players with their endorsements when they get in trouble. They strip them of all endorsements and hurt their pockets. I see how it feels on a much smaller scale. I felt heartbroken and betrayed. Why are the media so pessimistic and why do they seem to harp on negative stories? I had to figure this out. So many times, we turn on the television to check the news to see what's going on in our city. The majority of the stuff we see is negative, but why? The answer is simple: Negativity sells!

The media is looking for a good story, and the best stories on the air waves are the negative stories. Even our favorite television shows consists of reality shows that are filled with drama and ignorance. Ann Howard has a blog with "Shocking Statistics" on Reality Television. According to her, "Statistics show that 1/3 of Americans spend much of their free time watching TV and of that, 67% are reality shows."

People become consumed in the media and reality shows to escape their own realities. In times where the economy is hurting, people tend to watch other people's problems to take their minds off of their own issues. Professionals in the media understand this phenomenon and continue to saturate their networks with situations that seem to be worse than ours.

The problem with the media, from my perspective, is that they tend to run with the first story that they get, which is usually negative. They don't do their research in detail because they are focused on being the first station on the scene to cover a negative, exciting story. A positive story just doesn't cut it as headline news. Think about it.

The media isn't just informing the public of the hottest story, they are priming the minds of the viewers and setting the tone of a possible criminal case. In the two seconds we watch that segment, we, the public, have already formed an option of the scrutinized individual.

I was featured on the news twice before this incident took place for something positive. As excited as I was to get on the news for my good deeds and accomplishments, it didn't catch the public's attention as much as the negative Santa shooting. I guess Santa Claus being chivalrous a few days before Christmas just doesn't sound as entertaining as "Shooting Santa" or "Santa Clause robbing a gas station" (as some reports even tried to say), or as punk rockers, Kottonmouth Kings, who were playing St. Andrews Hall, that night, put it: "Crazy Santa goes on shooting spree outside Big Ballers event in Detroit. Our prayers are with the victims."

"Victims huh?!" I shouted. "How are they trying to act like the victims and they attacked us?!" I just couldn't understand it. Where did they get this artificial story? One news station also claimed that two off-duty officers had a foot chase with Santa, whom they ended up arresting. But I wasn't being chased by any cops, or was I?

According to the media, I was being chased by these off-duty cops who I thought at the time were the Arabian men. They were at the scene, and one claimed to have seen it all. But were there cops at the scene? Why didn't they intervene? There were more questions than answers. After all of the confusion and uncertainties, I had to regroup because, in less than 24 hours, Christmas was coming.

As I woke up Christmas morning, my daughter was super excited. She opened her gifts, but something was uneasy about her demeanor. She was happy about her new toys, but she couldn't enjoy them because of my facial expressions. I looked completely out of it. My first Christmas with her turned out to be my worst Christmas. Kids are smart. They know when something is wrong.

Her facial expressions reminded me of her confusion during the tormenting custody battle I had with her mother. She didn't know what was going on, but she suspected that something was wrong. Once again, her daddy was being portrayed as a villain, but this time, not through the venom of her mother's mouth, but through the animosity coming through the media outlets.

Fox 2 News was first on the scene for the coverage of my story, but they didn't realize the person who they were getting ready to bash with negative slandering was the guy on their station two months ago. Nevertheless, they jumped the gun on putting out a false story and using the most incriminating picture they could find of me. The Santa suit just made the perfect story. This just proved my theory of media jumping the gun and being so anxious to get a good story. I wasn't ready to give in yet.

It was time for me to strike back and defend my name. My pastor contacted his friend, Pastor David Bullock of Greater St. Matthew Baptist Church. As an activist throughout the city of Detroit, Pastor Bullock had established himself as a media sensation with a loyal fan base. He was a star on the reality television show called *Preachers of Detroit*.

Pastor Bullock called a press conference at his church on my behalf. The day of the press conference, he wore a brown, pinstriped suit. With his black, thick-rimmed glasses, he looked like a modern-day Malcolm X. Pastor Bullock, along with Pastor Bell, my mother, my father and Jasmine (Mrs. Claus), all made statements supporting me. They repudiated the earlier claims made by the media. Pastor Bullock went as far as to call me a "Super Santa" and asked for the charges to be dropped.

Jasmine then made a few statements, but was very careful not to talk about the case. She just stated the fact that I was there to help her with her tire and how it became a situation where she felt threatened. She summed it up by saying that if I wasn't there, she didn't know what would have happened that night.

My mother had gotten herself together well enough to make a few comments. "I'm glad I'm not at a funeral," she pronounced. "Rather, I'm here trying to defend my son. At least he still has breath in his body." Of course, the media wanted to interview me also, but my lawyer made it clear that I was off limits.

I hid in the car in my mom's back seat. The cameramen walked right past me as they were leaving the church. I had to be low key because media loves to rush you with mics and cameras even though you tell them not to.

Shortly thereafter, my pastor went on every radio station discussing my case. The radio station 107.5 FM was covering my story. I couldn't say anything about the case, but my pastor could say what he wanted. At this point, I still never made an official statement. My pastor defended me by telling my side of the story.

My phone started blowing up instantly. "Bro, they talking about you on the radio," one friend said. The station even had an open line for people to call in and give their input. Callers really say stupid stuff when they don't have all the facts. Comments like, "Why he wearing a Santa suit with a gun?" Obviously, I had to be at some sort of Christmas event. Everyone wanted to know why I ran from the scene. My pastor responded by saying I was being chased. But the news had the story like this, "Runaway, shooting Santa is captured by police on foot." I even heard some reports saying I drove away!

I had people calling the news stations on my behalf as well. The public opinion started to change in my favor. The good media ploy seemed to be working. Now, let me be clear. The good guy image was a good story because it brings a twist to the shooting Santa scenario. It wasn't that the media felt bad and wanted to help me get my story out. The headlines changed from "Crazy Santa shoots 2 in Detroit fight over Mrs. Claus" (New York Daily, 2014) to "Detroit Santa Shooter: Hero or villain" (Fox 2, 2014). It was just good TV.

Needless to say, with more media attention, my smart, little 5-year-old began to pick out my name and associate it with the situation. She asked me, "Daddy, did you shoot Santa?" That was the most awkward moment of my life. How do I explain this to her?

I just sat there silently shaking my head. That's all I could do. What could I say? Then it came to me. I looked at her and said, "No, baby, Daddy didn't shoot Santa. Daddy is a hero and he saved someone from getting shot." In the words of Pastor Bullock, "Daddy's a Super Santa."

My attempt to mitigate the situation only seemed to throw fuel on the fire. I would soon find out that the Prosecutor's office didn't take well to high profile cases. In fact, it seemed to motivate Kym Worthy, the Wayne County Prosecutor, to try even harder to prosecute me. It appeared to me that prosecutors were all about making a name for themselves or possibly getting a promotion. It's the same for judges and lawyers, too, I think.

My life was now a chess game. I was on their chess board and now it was their move. I wondered why Blacks were subject to incarcerations more often than other races. Are we naturally born criminals or are we subject to systemic failure? We need more positive stories being pushed in order to change the negative perceptions about us.

The images you see on social media, the news, and on movies promote the stereotype that Black people are violent criminals. However, the rate of Black college graduates has improved by three percentage points over the past two years. I found this on a website that explained statistics from the Journal of Blacks in Higher Education (www.jbhe.com). More encouraging is the fact that over the past seven years, the Black student graduation rate has improved at almost all of the nation's highest-ranked universities. This isn't heavily circulated through the media as it should be.

Obviously, I've been stereotyped before. I used to fit the stereotype of what the media called "thugs" in the eyes of some Americans. With the braids and urban clothes I wore, I was targeted plenty of times. My outfits and hairstyles mimicked my environment and the images I saw on TV.

I was an Allen Iverson fan at the time. He made braids and tattoos look cool to all teens in the late 90s. Eventually the look became an epidemic. For millionaire entertainers, it was cool, but for high school teenagers looking for employment, it was viewed as the common stereotypical look of a profiled gangster. No one wanted to hire kids with tattoos on their neck and face, or braids for that matter. I eventually cut them off after high school.

Glorifying drug dealing, calling women "hoes" while popping Percocet's and drinking lean has been subconsciously normalized throughout the music. There are not many conscious storytellers left in the Hip Hop Community. The Tupac's, the KRS 1's and the Bone Thugs in Harmony are now a dying breed. The question has to be raised in the Black community: how much of this injurious behavior should this new rap community take responsibility for? Is true Hip Hop dead?

Reality shows dejected music has not only glorified the thug mentality, but has desensitized drug addiction which, in return, is killing our community. The entertainment industry has made Black problems the number one selling product in urban America. The images people see are not convincing America that we are not the problem, but instead fortifying it.

I've read posts stating that some Americans feel that George Zimmerman's mindset was a mindset of being aware of his surroundings. They argue that as long as Blacks continue to perpetuate the thug mentality with pride, while the Black community as a whole does nothing to combat it, we will continue to be profiled as a whole.

Now, I know that media has perpetuated Blacks as a problem way before rap music ever existed. It just seems that now that we are able to capitalize off of the stereotype, we feel it's okay. Are we exacerbating the issue of profiling instead of mitigating it? It is a deep, honest question I found myself asking when I became a media target.

To make matters worse, the gas station videotape was not working. Without that tape, it would be my word versus theirs. There was no other gun found at the scene, according to the news. But what was very interesting was that the gas station clerk was interviewed by channel 7 and he claimed that there were shots fired from the black car towards the man (referring to me), which meant that it was a shootout that night. Someone was shooting at me and hopefully this clerk can describe what exactly happened that night. My life depended on it.

CHAPTER 6
Not the Judge, Too?!

"Oh well, if every young man of color is either a gang-banger or a thug, how hard is it to get them all mixed up?"

– Mike Weisser, Huffington Post

"Mr. Weldon, I'm shocked to see you here," the judge said during my first hearing. I found out later that the judge initially assigned to my case was a former prosecutor. So, while he was an elected official, his mentality was that of a prosecutor. I just didn't see how he was being neutral or waiting for facts. Instead, he was like everyone else in this crazy system... against me and the statement about his shock to see me left me mentally debilitated. I expected the prosecutor to make a statement like that, but not the judge, too!

Court can be very scary when you are fighting for your life. I think everyone has had some type of court experience rather its traffic court, civil court or even family court. I had my share of traffic cases and, of course, I had my custody cases. However, when it comes to fighting for your life in criminal court, it's a different ball game. Listening to two attorneys go back and forth trying to prove their point to a sometimes biased judge feels like complete strangers are playing ping pong with your life.

Two weeks of back and forth media attention was just the beginning of this mountain to climb. I had questions. What was the next step? What will happen at my next court date? Dennis, my attorney, had to explain to me that a preliminary hearing, preliminary examination, evidentiary hearing or probable cause hearing has to happen next. I didn't even know what a preliminary examination was!

I had to look up on Wikipedia, which stated, "It is a proceeding, after a criminal complaint has been filed by the prosecutor, to determine whether there is enough evidence to require a trial. The judge must find that such evidence provides probable cause to believe that the crime was committed by the defendant." Yep. That was me.

Dennis also told me that he received some scary news. One of the guys I had shot was in critical condition and it wasn't looking good for him. He had a 50/50 chance of survival. So, the prosecutor had asked if my bond should be raised higher or if I should even have a bond at all. If this man dies, it becomes a murder case! Then, I would be picked back up and locked back up with possibly no bond. In other words, after my next court date, I may not be coming home from court, but back to the horrendous, intimidating County Jail!

Certainly, that didn't sit too well with me. For the next two nights, I took two sleeping pills along with anxiety medicine to force myself to get some rest. Honestly, I didn't care if I woke up the next day. I was distressed.

The next morning, I got dressed and headed out

the door. "Let's get this over with," I said to myself. I jumped into the car and drove to the court house. As I pulled up and parked, I saw the news trucks in front of the building along with police cars. I walked up to the building with my head high until I saw 40 or more family members of one of the "victims" standing in front of the building looking at me. To get through the doors, I would have to get past them.

I was by myself and saw no familiar faces in the crowd. I didn't even see my mom or dad. I was by myself as I started to walk through the crowd. The Arabian males started spitting on me and swearing at me! And then...... Buzzzzzz!!! My alarm clock went off. It was just a dream! These were the types of dreams, or should I say nightmares, that I was having every night. But it was time for court and time to man up.

My second court date was Thursday, January 8, 2015, in Detroit, Michigan. I got dressed very slowly that morning. My legs felt like jello pudding pops. I could hardly stand up straight. I knew this was going to be a horrible experience. I knew that judge was going to lock me up this time.

I called friends and put the courtroom number and the time to show up on my Facebook page. I needed support. I needed to fill the courtroom again. I know after seeing all my friends in the courtroom last time, the plaintiff's family would come in deep... very deep.

As we got into the car, my mom told me that she couldn't go this time because it was too much on her. If she were to see me get arrested, it would destroy her. I drove with my dad and a few church members to the Frank Murphy Hall of Justice. Without a doubt, this was the longest ride of my life.

As we pulled up to the court house, we saw the media trucks outside waiting and reporting. I walked up to the door with my family. It took a while to get in the building. The line was so long. Not to mention, it was freezing cold outside. After all, it was January in Michigan. I felt like a chocolate icicle by the time I made it inside.

The metal detectors looked like the ones I remembered in high school, but instead of security guards around them, there were a lot of sheriffs and German shepherd dogs. I wondered how they would react if I gave them my business card for the LaGuard Vest. The product would be perfect for their training. They would probably look at me like I was crazy.

When I see dogs, my mind immediately goes into marketing mode for the LaGuard product. That's how my cousin and I trained our thinking. "You see dogs? Get ready to pitch the product. It's sell time!" we would say. *"Now how in the world could I be thinking about selling products at a time like this? I may not even be leaving out of here tonight,"* I said to myself. I suppose that was a good sign that I had not lost who I was yet. I was an entrepreneur regardless of what the media says.

After getting searched, I proceeded upstairs to the courtroom. I could see friends and family coming in the building through the metal detectors behind me. Even through the cold, my friends, co-workers and church family were showing up to support me. That gave me hope.

I must admit, I was quite surprised at who showed up for me. The people who showed up were people I didn't expect. They were people who I didn't think cared that much about me. The people I expected didn't show up. I saw co-workers, friends I hadn't seen in years, my pastor and my church family. Sometimes even people who feel like strangers can be your biggest supporters. When you're in a situation like this, you need people to show up and support you. It makes a hell of a difference!

In front of the courtroom was another story. The hallways were full of the plaintiff's family and friends. Some in suits looking like lawyers and some in street clothes. I found myself thinking about them in line with a common stereotype for people of Middle Eastern descent. *"They look like ISIS!"* I thought.

The hallway was full of people of Middle Eastern descent and I found myself enslaved to the news and propaganda. Every news station on CNN or Fox television stations depict terrorists as Arabs. I was terrified when I walked up to the courtroom door. *"So, they gotta be terrorists!"* I assumed. Unfortunately, people would have a similar, judgmental reaction if they saw a group of Black people walk in the courtroom with street clothes. We would be considered thugs or from the ghetto.

It's not right, but the media has tainted our minds, and I honestly felt bad to even think that. I was angry at them for what they did to us. It looked like every gas station owner and party store owner was in the courtroom! I was upset at the fact that we had to spend money at their gas stations and at their stores and we, as Blacks, were nothing but consumers and had no power in the community. I had to remind myself that everyone of Middle Eastern descent isn't an owner of one of those establishments and they all aren't bad, but my mind was racing so fast. For the first time in my life, I felt like a racist.

We all began to enter the courtroom and between both of our families and friends, we filled the entire court room. I was proud to say that the prison guard was wrong. The Arabian people were together and my family stuck together. The media took pictures of the scene. It was a sight to see.

Now the fun part comes in waiting hours before your court case is called and you see a lot of action while you wait. The court cases called before mine were interesting. Being able to watch all those cases you learn something. You learn how the system really has control over so many lives.

Drug charge after drug charge poured in. Young Black men were walking in and out with their pants hanging and looking like me in high school. Most of them were much older than I was when I had that mindset. I was 17 then, but the guys I saw come in court that day were from ages 24 to 32.

They had no guidance whatsoever. They had no type of court etiquette or court dress attire. I could tell because they were by themselves, only accompanied by their attorneys. They had no type of support—no family and no friends. This was what the prison guard was referring to.

"That's probably why they are in the courtroom in the first place," I presumed.

As time went on, I could feel the anticipation building up for my case. The sounds and whispers around the courtroom sounded like a customer service call center. There was an anxiousness and hostility in the air. People were upset. Their demeanors were very negative. No one really got out of hand. Everyone was respectful, but eager to get started.

The media began setting up their cameras and then, in walked my attorney. He called me over to talk in private. As I stood up, I could no longer see my family, but only a sea of angry Arabian men. The courtroom was full of the plaintiff's family. They all watched me as I got up and walked outside to talk to Dennis.

You could tell the Arabians were well connected. The only people allowed in the court rooms with cell phones are people who worked for the Frank Murphy court house. The Arabians in suits had their phones out texting and calling people. "How are they doing that?" I wondered.

These men were going in the back with the Prosecutor and even speaking to my attorney a few times. "What the hell are they talking to him about?" I wondered. "Look at all of these gas station owners!" I scoffed. The courtroom was filled with Arabian men with unknown occupations, but, of course, my stereotyping continued. I felt like I had got into a beef with the mob.

"The driver who was shot in the hand will take the stand first and then the police officer who claimed to have seen it all will be next. The detective is still looking for the clerk to interview him and get him to testify," Dennis explained privately. He let me know to get ready because my case was starting in a few minutes.

I went into the restroom to throw water on my face. A police officer walked in. He looked so familiar to me, but I couldn't put a finger on where I had seen him. The officer was a dark-skinned, heavy set man who was wearing his uniform. He had a young face so he was probably in his early 30s. He kind of reminded me of the cartoon character, Fat Albert. The crazy thing was that he refused to look at me in the eye, like he was hiding something. I didn't think much of it and proceeded to get back to the courtroom to get ready for my case to start.

Those next few seconds of waiting were more like minutes. The bailiff finally called my case, "Calling case 14-65965 People of the State of Michigan vs. Marcus Allen Weldon. Mr. Weldon is charged with 7 counts." This would be the second time that I would hear all those charges read off and each time my body trembled because of the excruciating anxiety of what would happened if I was declared guilty.

The Prosecutor began her introduction. "Good morning, your Honor. Klan Capers on behalf of the People," she stated matter-of-factly. She was a middle-aged white woman with long, blond hair who looked like she had a hard life. She was wearing a dark gray suit and an ace bandage on one of her arms. She looked as if she hadn't slept in 5 days because there were heavy bags under her eyes.

Dennis then proceeded with his introduction. "Good morning, your Honor. Dennis Craig on behalf of Marcus Weldon who is standing to my right." I looked to my far left to see the prosecutor. Once again, I was always trying to read people to see what I was up against. Dennis continued with a summary of the case and indicated that the gas station clerk still had not been found.

We had hired a private detective to find the clerk who worked at the gas station. He was scared and didn't want to be interviewed. He told my attorney on the phone that he didn't want anything to do with the case, however, he was the one person that said that there was a shootout that night. He and Jasmine were my only two witnesses. The crazy part was that he no longer worked at the gas station and he also moved out of the city.

Dennis argued, "Your Honor, the defense is making a request for a continuance of the preliminary examination. I think it's a good faith request here. The defense wants to bring an eyewitness to court who shows that there was more than one firearm that was used in this case and that my client was defending himself at the time when this occurred. As you remember when we were in court the other day, I received a witness statement from Akmed Mohammed who worked at the gas station where this occurred. And, upon reading his statement, I saw that it said that although the person in the Santa Claus suit was shooting, he also says that he heard shots from the direction that the Arabian guy ran to."

This made sense to me. I heard shots from the car, so maybe the driver was the one shooting. All I kept thinking was, "But, where is their gun and why wasn't it found?" My attorney stated that the clerks contact information was redacted by the prosecutor's office, which included his addresses and phone number. Now, why would the prosecutor hide his information from my lawyer?

My attorney wanted to put him on the witness stand, but the prosecutor's office appeared to be blocking him. They told him they would give the clerk his phone number and have him call my attorney himself. But at that point, no one had contacted him.

The prosecutor responded, "He's had the clerk's name and statement since before Christmas when discovery was made available when the defendant was charged. Mr. Craig knows where he is. He's at the gas station." Then, she admitted she couldn't contact him either.

I could tell that the prosecutor was ready to get the ball rolling on this case. She couldn't wait to put the "victim" on the stand to testify against me. I glanced over at him. He had metal rods in his arm, which was wrapped in a sling. She wanted to proceed without one of my key witnesses. That couldn't be good for me.

Fortunately, Dennis was ready and he counter-argued, "I anticipated she would make that argument. That's why I have my private investigator here, your Honor, whom I sent to the gas station between the last court date and today. He was told that that man no longer works there. Now it's either A.) it's a lie by them because they don't want us talking to him, or B.) maybe he doesn't. That's why I needed that contact information."

The Judge compromised by saying, "If you want

that witness, you can get that info and you can bring him back another date." At that point, my lawyer and the prosecutor agreed to move on with the proceedings.

Dennis brought up another issue that some information from a police report was redacted about the victims. "I believe that that's criminal history and that I have the right to have," Dennis argued. This meant that the two guys both had something on their criminal record, possibly felonies or misdemeanors. Whatever it was, these guys were not angels.

The judge seemed to get irritated and said, "You don't have a right to get lien counsel!" It was almost like he was working with the prosecutor in hiding something. I started to see how well my attorney knows the law. He argued his point with the judge quoting precedence from Supreme Court case states and vying for equal footing with the prosecutor.

Finally, after the back and forth, the Judge asked both the attorneys to come to front and have a private talk off the record. As the attorneys walked to the back room to talk with the judge, the room went silent. It was so quiet that you could hear a pen drop. I could feel everyone's eyes burning through my back, staring me down. The news cameras snapped more pictures as they waited for the case to continue. Click! Click! Click! Click!

I picked up a folder in front of me. I was shaking uncontrollably. I quickly dropped the paper on the table. I didn't want anyone to see me sweat, especially the news reporters. It's like they were waiting for me to breakdown. I couldn't show any emotion. I couldn't let them know how sick I really was. I felt dehydrated and weak.

"What are they talking about back there?" I wondered. It felt like they were back there for thirty minutes, but in reality, it was more like three minutes. I wanted to turn around so bad and look at my dad's face, but that meant I would also be looking at the Plaintiffs' families' faces. I couldn't look to the left because the media was watching and taking pictures. I couldn't look to the right of me because there were guys that looked like sheiks who wanted me locked up or dead. So, I stared straight ahead and waited.

Finally, they walked back into the courtroom. The Judge told my lawyer that there isn't anything that could be used for purpose of impeachment or anything of that nature so let's move on. The prosecutor then proceeded to talk about the second guy who was shot. He was still at the hospital with a tube in his throat and was on oxygen. But the other victim was there and ready to testify.

The court called the driver who was shot in the hand to the stand. The prosecutor began asking him questions like what he was doing before the shooting, where he worked and how well he knew the other victim. Through these questions I learned some more information. They worked together at another gas station in Detroit that one of their brothers owned.

"See!" I thought, *"They all either work at a gas station or they own one!"* They were also neighbors and decided to go out riding to check out gas prices. He said they went downtown to cruise and stop at the gas station to get some water.

"Is he serious?" I said to myself. *"Who drives around looking at gas prices, ends up downtown cruising and then stops for water at 2 o'clock in the morning? I know the Judge isn't going to believe this story! Or is he?"* He also stated that his boy left the door cracked open when he got out of the car, which was another lie. I remember it was wide open. I could see straight into the car.

I remember the driver talking back and forth to his partner while digging around looking for something. He stated his boy stepped back trying to get his attention and accidentally bumped her. Then, he claimed that I stepped into his face. He claimed his friend never put his hands on me. It was just a shouting match. That is not how I remembered it!

The prosecutor continued the interrogation, "Are you aware that the officers wrote down that you said your friend came back to the car to try and get a bat?"

"Yeah, I read it," the Plaintiff responded.

"Do you remember saying that to the officer?"

"I probably did. I was terrified, I was in shock. I mean, I didn't think my boy was going to make it."

This guy was doing a lot of guessing. How can you get away with guessing anything in the courtroom? My attorney objected to several things he stated, "He can't be guessing anything." The Judge rolled his eyes like a little girl. It was obvious that he was getting tired of my attorney objecting. I wished he would quit listening to this bull crap. What a liar this guy is!

I haven't even made an official statement and Jasmine hasn't taken the stand yet either. This guy is pathetic. In my opinion, the only thing he said that was the truth was his name. I guess I just started shooting for no reason.

He finished by saying "I got out the car to check on my friend and call 911. Then someone came up and said, 'Lay down. I'm a police officer.' I waited for the EMS truck and never moved again."

This was horrible. *"When do I get to speak? I can't take it!"* I was yelling in my mind. I remembered, I wanted to jump up and tell my side of the story. But I had to stay calm and ride it out. It was time for my lawyer to cross-examine him and catch him up in these lies.

Dennis began asking him miscellaneous questions like what his name was and how old he was. He asked if he had been drinking or smoking marijuana that night and if he had ever been convicted of a felony or a misdemeanor. Of course, the Plaintiff gave the impression that he was the cleanest thing in the courtroom. His story was the same about checking gas prices, but he couldn't seem to remember any of the prices. Something wasn't right, but I was looking at the Judge's face as the Plaintiff told his story and I could tell that the Judge was believing everything he said.

Dennis continued, "I ask you again, how did Kareem shove my client?"

"I don't know. I mean... I seen some of it."

"And, wasn't it true that a gun was pulled to back Kareem off my client?"

"I don't know what he was trying to do."

"And at that point in time after the gun was simply pulled

out, isn't it true that you told the police that Kareem went back to the car and tried to get a bat?

"I was guessing. I mean, the police talked to me at that moment I was guessing that. I was in shock."

"That doesn't mean you lie!"

This guy is unbelievable! He admitted he was guessing about a lot of things. There was, in fact, shoving before any guns were pulled out. There was no bat. He told the 911 operator he didn't see who shot him, but now he's saying he saw me shoot him. He was just pissed. *"I don't care if he was shot in the arm, that doesn't mean you can just lie,"* I thought to myself. This story was getting crazier and crazier as we went along.

Gradually my mind started to drift. I couldn't hear anything in the courtroom. I could only hear my heart beating. I thought I was going to have a heart attack. This was too much going back and forth. Why does it feel like the witness gets away with lies? Why doesn't the video tape work? These are legitimate questions. I am the victim here, not this man.

It was finally time to switch to a new witness. The off-duty police officer who claimed he was at the scene walked in. I paused for a second and then it hit me. *"That's the cop I saw in the bathroom earlier today. No wonder he couldn't look me in the eye! Something isn't right,"* I thought.

The prosecutor questioned him first, asking him his name, where he served as a police officer, where he was the night of the incident and who was with him. He answered that he was an officer for the City of Detroit and that he was off duty that night. He came to the gas station with another officer in a black Ford, which was a personal vehicle.

So, this was the black car that followed me from the gas station. At the time, I thought it was the two thugs I had the altercation with. It's a blessing that I didn't shoot at that car. This could have really gone south! I recall that I was seconds away from turning around and using my firearm on that black car following us. If I had done that, I would have shot these two police officers. Can you imagine what the story would have been then? "Santa Shoots Two Unarmed Men and Two Off Duty Cops." That was God telling me not to shoot them.

The cop took the stand:

"I overheard arguing from the building. I couldn't hear what was being said, but just raised voices. I saw the defendant in an altercation with an Arabian man in front of the cashier's window. After some pushing and shoving, I saw the Middle Eastern male walking back to his car. Then, I saw the defendant pulling a weapon from his right side and then firing shots in the direction of the Middle Eastern man."

"How many shots did you hear?" The prosecutor asked.

"I don't recall how many shots there were, but after the shots stopped, I saw the defendant running across the gas station parking lot dragging a light-skinned female behind him."

From the cops' testimony, it sounded like I shot the man while he was running to the car, which would have meant that he was shot in the back. This was not true. He was shot in the stomach; so how do you explain that?

It was my attorney's chance to cross-examine the officer.

"Officer, may we see your written report or notes on this incident?"

"I'm not sure where they are." The officer admitted. "The last time I saw them was the night I wrote them. I'm sure I threw them in the garbage," he said.

"You destroyed them, in other words" Dennis asked.

"Yes," he replied.

"Who does that?" my attorney replied.

The officer's testimony was peculiar: First, the time he arrived on the scene seems sketchy. He says he saw some things, but in his call to 911, he reported something differently, which he didn't recall. He saw me with a gun, but he didn't see anybody else with a gun. He didn't see anybody else in the Arabian's Dodge Charger. He followed me when I ran away from the gas station for a few feet and then called 911. He spoke with other officers about what happened and added some of that conversation to his testimony even though he didn't witness it. I could see why he wouldn't look me in the eye.

When the off-duty officer was given permission to step down from the witness stand, the Judge and the lawyers discussed setting up another court date after the clerk could be found. "So we'll adjourn this matter or continue this matter on January 15. I'm sorry. You wanted to…"

the Judge paused and the prosecutor stepped forward.

"Your Honor, the People noted on Monday in discussion with your Honor and Mr. Craig that we thought bond was low in this matter." The prosecutor argued to the judge that because the Plaintiffs had several injuries and that one of the "victim's" father passed away, and in light of the evidence presented that day, the bond should be increased. Now, the only reason to increase a bond is to put somebody in jail because they can't pay it. I was horrified.

My lawyer objected to that request and pointed out reasons why my bond shouldn't be increased. I was 26-years-old. I had no criminal history. I had a valid CPL permit to carry a gun. I was an electrical engineer apprentice at the casino and have been working there for six years. I had full custody of my 5-year-old daughter. Dennis had 20 or 30-character letters from different community members of good character and mentioned that my whole church was strongly behind me.

The Judge seemed to be seriously contemplating increasing my bond. "There are a number of things that the court must consider when considering the departure from the state bond. And those are the same conditions that are considered when the initial bond is imposed. And some of the more important things are: danger to the community, risk of flight, likelihood of conviction and I'll stop there because those are the major ones," the Judge stated matter-of-factly.

Dennis really went to bat for me with the Judge on this one, but the Judge gave the impression that he believed everything the Plaintiff and the off-duty cop said. I shook my head in disbelief. "Sir, you don't get to comment either," the Judge said to me. "You don't get to look at me and shake your head and say no to me. You get to sit there and talk to your counsel. If you want to testify you can take the stand, sir, but you do not testify from that table." This was awful. In court, you can't even so much as shake your head in disagreement without being held in contempt. I wanted this day to be over.

After further discussion with Dennis, the Judge asked if he could "voir dire" me. A voir dire is a preliminary examination of a witness or a juror by a judge or counsel. The decision of my bond was about to be left up to me.

The Judge asked me my age, where I went to school, where I lived, who I lived with and if I had a lot of community support. I answered his questions and he said, "This makes it even more sad, sir. That you are a young man with so much potential and something that could be offered."

"Yes, your Honor," I agreed with him. "I understand how it sounds, sir, and it's a lot more to the story."

"I don't want you to say anything that's not prompted by me. So, I pick my questions very carefully, sir," the Judge scolded me.

"Sorry," I replied sorrowfully.

The Judge went on to ask me what church I attended and when was the last time I went. Fortunately, I really do attend church faithfully and was there the previous Sunday.

"It's very disturbing evidence that I've heard today, Mr. Weldon. So, tell you what I'm going to do. Because this is subject to change based on what's going to happen next. Because right now…"

The Judge paused for what seemed like 35 days, but it was more like 35 seconds. It was the longest 35 seconds of my life. I didn't know what he was going to say. It looked like my options were either jail, a higher bond or going home.

"Will you just come out with it? Let's get this over with!" I yelled at the judge.

Ok, I didn't yell at the judge, but if I had, that's what I would have said. I held my breath and I froze up just like I had several times that day. All I could hear were my thoughts and my heart beating.

He finally spoke and I could breathe again. "I'm going to give you a tether. And your movements are going to be stricken." A tether? Really? Good grief. *"Well,"* I thought. *"That's better than jail. Anything is better than the County."*

The Judge allowed me to pick my daughter up from school, attend school at nights, and go to church on Sundays. I could only be out of my house Monday through Saturday from 2:30 p.m. to 10:45 p.m. and on Sunday 8:30 a.m. to 3:00 p.m. The Judge finally declared, "This matter is adjourned until January 15th." I wanted to crawl under the table and wait until the courtroom was completely cleared out. Forget speaking to anyone. When your life is in the palm of someone else's hands like that, you can barely breathe.

CHAPTER 7
House Arrest!

"The electronic monitoring people are like old-fashioned bounty hunters. It's a newfangled debtors' prison."

– Jack Duncan, a public defender in Richland County, South Carolina

House arrest! "What just happened?" I distressingly wondered as I walked out of the courtroom. The Judge put me on house arrest. I went from being a commodity to the community to a pending criminal and treated like some kind of menace to society. My stipulations on tether were unbearably strict.

I only had enough time to get my daughter from school and go to class in the evenings. I couldn't get any action on Saturday, and if I violated any of these conditions, my bond would be revoked and I would be sent back to jail. Now, I'm used to going out of town and constantly moving. Remember, I was always busy and working. At the moment, I had to sit down and regroup. I was an emotional wreck. I had never been in this position before.

I just couldn't believe that cop freestyled that fabricated story and the Judge sided with the lying "victim." In reality, no one had taken the stand on my behalf yet.

I haven't even made an official statement. The Judge was only going on what he heard, and the police officer sealed the deal with his inaccurate statements. The prosecutor really wanted me back in jail with a higher bond, but the Judge didn't throw me in jail. Thank God for a little bit of justice!

The crowd surrounded me like a mob when I left out of the courtroom. Everyone was talking at the same time. Everything sounded like distorted noise. The media camera men rushed in on me and began snapping pictures and asking questions.

Click! Click! Click! Click! The flashes blinded me for a few seconds as I looked for my family. It was like the Grammy's, only this was not a celebration. It was a nightmare. This fortuitous situation of chivalry was now a disaster. My life was officially upside down.

I quickly found a safe area in the stairwell avoiding all the cameras and questions. I needed to think and map out my next move. My attorney got stopped and was questioned by a Fox 2 news reporter, but after he spoke to the media, he joined me in the stairwell.

"We made out pretty good considering the Judge could have locked you back up," he said. "These charges were serious and the Judge wasn't happy after what he heard in the courtroom today." Dennis told me we had another court date in two weeks and hopefully the gas station clerk could be located by then. My next stop was to the William Dickerson Detention Facility to get my new court-issued accessory.

On the way out, the courthouse people began to

voice their opinions. "Why hasn't he put Jasmine on the stand? Why haven't you spoken yet? Where you get him at?" One problem I was beginning to encounter was that everyone thought they were attorneys and experts in criminal law. Most of them have never even been to court for even as much as a traffic ticket. I began to block people's opinions out in order to keep a sane mind. "I love you and thanks for your support, but I'm following my lawyer's lead," I told them all.

Family support is a double-edged sword. Sometimes they're ignorant and insensitive comments bring you down and frustrate you, but it's only out of love. I couldn't take it personally. In any case, you have to know the difference between those who have your best interest at heart and those who are just nosey as hell.

I was being called the "Santa Claus Shooter." You can imagine how many nosey people appeared on my Caller I.D. My case was on television and my face was on every local news channel and social media blog. Like I said earlier, my business was everyone's business.

As I pulled up to the Dickerson Detention Facility, I could feel the tension in the air. The street was full of potholes. The brown building looked like an old college campus being used as a prison. It was surrounded by Oakland County Sheriff's cars.

My father dropped me off at the door. He couldn't come in with me, but he left me with some encouraging words. "Remember, you were built for this. You're strong," he said. I gave him a small smile and proceeded to the door.

The first thing I saw was a sign on the door that said, "No friends, family members or cell phones allowed inside." I was on my own. With trembling hands, I reached for the cold steel door handle.

Inside that building was something else. There was a small room divided by an electrical power metal door. On my right was a thick glass wall and sitting behind that glass was an older Black gentlemen. He asked me for my paperwork. I handed it to him through the hole cut out at the bottom of the glass. He told me to sit down on the wooden bench in front of the window.

Instantly, the power door slid open. The sound of metal screeching across the floor as it began to slide open was like eighteen keys going across the side of a car door. I stood up from the bench and waited for about five minutes and then proceeded to walk in.

A man came out of nowhere yelling at me. "Did I tell you to walk through my doors?" It was the same man from behind the glass window. This was my first time here so I didn't know what to do. *"Excuse me, sir! What is the normal procedure?"* I wanted to ask, but I kept my mouth shut. When the doors opened, I assumed it was time to step up and go in. I wasn't given any other instructions. I didn't understand it then, but later I learned that this hazing was all part of the dehumanizing of recidivism. When you are in the system, you lose your human rights, which included respect.

I didn't argue with him. I backed up and went back to the bench and sat down, at which point he said, "Ok, now step up and come in." Really? I guess he was used to dealing with stupid, guilty people. I'm not one of them. In fact, I'm technically innocent until proven guilty, but obviously this is a paradox. It's more like guilty until proven innocent.

The man then ordered me to take everything out my pockets and walk through the metal detectors slowly. He was very militant in his approach and I was still shell-shocked from my court appearance. How much more of this can I take?

"Go sit down on the wooden bench and wait," he instructed. So I went. I sat there for three hours before someone else came out to give me further instructions. For those three hours, I had to get a grip on myself.

I felt a little claustrophobic in this cold and dark hallway with tables and benches. On the far end of the hallway was another sliding door. Directly in front of me was a door that looked like it led to the office space. This is where the militant gentlemen went and stayed for three hours.

The whole time I day-dreamed, trying to take my mind off of my situation and think positively, but it was hard to be positive in this ice-cold, empty hallway. My head felt at least a hundred pounds heavier as I struggled to hold it upright sitting at the bench waiting. I just knew my neck would break! All of my miracles and blessings that had occurred in the last few years in my life meant nothing. I was losing myself in this dreadful mess.

Without warning, a younger, dark skinned man came out of the door in front of me. He had on all black with a gun on his hip and police badge. He told me to follow him. "Follow me," he said, in a flat, but persistent tone. We walked to the end of the hallway and entered through the other set of sliding doors, which led into another long hallway of rooms.

We walked quietly not saying a word to each other. Each person that I had encountered thus far in this place, had a flat and rough demeanor about them. This place not only dehumanizes the inmates and criminals, but it robotized the guards into nonsocial creatures with no compassion. It fills them with a sense of detachment from human life. The prison system affects everyone involved, even its own employees.

We finally arrived in a room which was full of inmates wearing blue jumpsuits. I found out that this was a prison as well, and inmates were everywhere mopping floors and wiping windows. This area was surrounded by single zone jail cells. The inmates were let out at certain times to clean up and mingle with each other. I had the misfortune of experiencing three incarceration facilities in a matter of weeks.

I was told to sit down amongst the inmates doing janitorial work and not to speak to anyone. But, from the moment I sat down, the questions from nosey inmates began to fire off. "What you do fam? You getting tha box?" I quickly found out that "the box" was the code name for the tether. I didn't respond to them, I just sat there looking off into space, waiting for my next direction from the officer.

Finally, after a half hour, the officer came back in the room and told me to come with him. He pointed to the wall and told me stand against the wall in front of a digital camera. This was not how I envisioned my last photo shoot would be. My new mug shot would soon be uploaded on Google for everyone to see.

After that, it was time to get "the box." I was taken back to the original hallway where this unbelievable saga began. I was given a packet of instructions to read about the tether. The thing that struck me was that the first page said that to be on tether is a privilege. I almost laughed. According to the Oxford Dictionary, a tether is "a rope or chain with which an animal is tied to restrict its movement." It's definitely not a privilege for an innocent man to be considered an animal and to have his movements restricted. *"I shouldn't even be getting this damn thing!"* I said to myself.

The officer who handed me the packet began to go over it with me telling me all the rules. I now had to check in once a week with my assigned officer. I had to charge the tether for two hours straight a day. If the charger was taken out before the two hours was up, I had to start the changing process over. In case you were wondering, you don't get to take it off to charge it. No! You have to stand or sit by an electrical outlet for two hours straight. Also, I didn't charge it while I was sleeping because the possibility of the charging chord coming out while I was asleep was too great.

The officer told me to put my leg up on the table. He then put on the tether, a black box with a speaker on it, around my ankle. It looked like an outdated version from the size of it. It was like one of those old walkie-talkies I used to play with back in the 90's. That thing was uncomfortable and felt like a heavy rubber water hose wrapped around my leg.

My privacy rights at home were now gone with this tether. The officer explained, "Since this is government's property, you are government's property." This meant that if they needed to come get it out of my house, they could with no warrant and if the tether was damaged it would cost me $1,500 to replace it.

I could take showers, but no baths because the device couldn't be submerged under water. I was also subject to routine checks and that little speaker on the side was an informant. They could hear everything I'm saying, so if they wanted to listen to me or speak to me they could do so at any time. It was prison inside my home; a direct extension of the County.

After I was adorned and fully educated on the box, I was led into a small office divided into cubicles. Tether officers were in each of them. Each tether officer had their own desk with a young Black male being processed through this house arrest enrollment.

There was a huge, 60-inch television screen with a GPS map on it. The little red dots represent the locations of the tether participants. The dots were in clusters all across the map of Detroit. You could actually see the dots moving around as the people moved from location to location. When I say they see your every move, that's an understatement. They actually see your movement in the house as you walk to the backyard to throw the trash away.

My stupefaction of the map with the moving, red lights was interrupted when I was introduced to my tether officer, Ms. Hall, a middle-aged Black woman who was very quiet at first. After a while, the attitude that comes along with working a job like that with the juveniles and rejects of society reared its ugly head. I can remember her smacking her gum as she repeated my schedule for the week and what would happen if I don't stick to the court order.

Ms. Hall explained that I would also have to pay $100 a month for this tether. One hundred dollars a month is not cheap for something that tracks your every move and keeps you in invisible bondage. This doesn't include lawyer fees, bond fees, private investigators or all of the stuff I had to do to beat the case.

She printed out a map that was the "no fly zone." This was an area that I couldn't go to because it was the area where the two guys or "victims" stayed. I was considered the aggressor in this situation and a danger to these guys. The area was actually a block away from the tether office. If I missed my turn and accidentally passed the office, I could have ended up in the no fly zone, which would have landed me back in jail.

My check-in date was set to the next Tuesday at 3:30 p.m. I was told to get home before curfew starts. I left out of the building with a damaged self-esteem. My thoughts were filled with shame and fear of the unknown. I was starting not to believe in myself. Doubt and worry blocked my faith and vision.

It was a long ride home with my dad. By this time,

my uncle had joined him and gave me some good advice. He was a former Detroit police officer and knew the ropes. He told me, "The media and jury will be watching your every move. Never shake your head in the courtroom or show emotions."

Too late for that piece of advice. I remember shaking my head at the very end of the first hearing when the Judge yelled at me. That was the only time I showed emotion. But I couldn't take it anymore. The pressure of the officer's artificial story made me hang my head and Fox 2 was right on it. In fact, when I got home, I was the subject of the top story on the "Let It Rip" Fox 2 debate.

CHAPTER 8
Alcohol, Shoes and Books

"The writer's gift can make us see ourselves and our morals differently than our reality suggests."

– Dr. Michael Eric Dyson

Fox 2's "Let it Rip" show was a very popular show in Detroit. The popular news anchor, Charlie Langton, hosts the show and is known to let his opinion "rip". My case was an interesting topic for Christmas. So they invited my Pastor, my friend, Sonya, and Rick Ector from *Legally Armed in Detroit* to the "Let it Rip" show. My father was invited, but refused because he was emotionally unstable and was afraid he may say the wrong thing and hurt my case.

My Pastor began telling my story. The show allows people to voice their opinion on social media via Twitter. Tweets began to flash across the screen for the viewers to read. The cyber bullies were back with their comments, but this time my support flooded the social media overshadowing the negative tweets with positive tweets.

Charlie questioned my pastor about the fact that there was no gun found at the scene. Pastor Bell told him that the scene was not roped off and the scene was not properly searched. This, of course, struck a nerve with the news anchors. No one wants to believe that police officers make mistakes or even lie. They get the benefit of doubt over the accused criminal in most cases, but the paradigm has been shifting as of late.

The criminal justice system has been under scrutiny with cases such as Sandra Bland, Philando Castile and Freddie Gray. But, of course, with the tape not working, the evidence is against me. The only thing I have going is my good character and Jasmine's testimony.

As I got up to turn the television off something caught my eye. The next debate coming up on "Let it Rip" was a debate on Arabian Muslim extremists and terrorism. It was kind of ironic that they put that debate right after mine, considering the fact that the two men I shot were of Arab descent. The guests on the show were Osama Siblani, a popular news anchor on the Arab American news station of Detroit, Imam Mohammad and Elahi the leader of Islamic house.

After they debated the topic of the growing terrorist threat, Osama said something very interesting. He switched gears and got off topic and vouched for the two young men that I had the altercation with. He said "I know those boys; they are good boys and they did not have guns."

Wow! I couldn't believe it. The cohesive culture, the bond they have between each other. Their people stick together no matter what. He got off topic to stick his neck out and reputation on the line for these guys. He probably really didn't even know them. But that showed me how important culture was. The importance of culture is that it brings a nationalistic agenda to the table, which means that the ethnic agenda of the people goes before anything else. Now I see that there is a difference between "color" and "ethnic identity." Who you identify yourself with has more to do with culture than color.

No matter the circumstances, they will stand by their people. It's like a brotherhood or fraternity. I have a friend who is Dominican and he has an automatic connection with anyone he meets who is Dominican because of his cultural connection. That cultural connection helps build rapport and commonality with a person.

The news anchors even questioned my pastor, "Why are you even putting your reputation on the line for him?" He told them because he knows my character and he's known me for years. My point here is that I was blessed to have my people backing me up in the time of crisis.

I knew a few news anchors personally. I knew that they wouldn't dare share their input on live television for me, in fear of backlash, just as my mentor at the Casino didn't stand up or call me back because of fear. Most cases for Blacks only get supporters when the "victim" or accused "suspect" is dead. And, once again, like the prison guard said, that the Arabian culture sticks together.

I began to look on Facebook for Osama Siblani's page and followed an article that had my picture I took at the tether office attached to it. My picture was on his Facebook page which was an Arabian news page so it was super biased. I was almost in tears reading some of the comments they wrote about me. I was the enemy to an entire ethnic group of people. It was like the "Black people vs. Arabian people". This easily could have had turned into a race war if we weren't careful.

I started therapy right after I got out of jail. The therapist recommended I take off work for a medical leave. He also gave me anxiety medication to help me deal. I was avoiding HR because there was too much media attention going on. That gave me additional time to let everything die down and get through the court procedures. I was hoping I would soon get back to my normal life. It didn't happen as soon as I had hoped.

When you're laying down at nighttime and thinking, it is the worst time without a doubt. It's just you, the tether and your thoughts. Charging the tether was a pain, as I slept with one leg propped up like I was in the hospital after ankle surgery. It was hard to stay woke for two hours by an outlet with this distorted cacophony going on in my head. The sound in my head was worse than the sound of car horns produced in a traffic jam during rush hour.

Then, I began to see the difference between true altruism and surreptitious selfishness. During the two-week point, everyone was calling and coming over. A lot of people showed up to court and even spoke on my behalf to the news. But who was genuine and who was doing it for five seconds of media attention?

In high-profile cases, it is hard to differentiate the people who care, the noisy people and the clandestine, and the egotistic media narcissists. If my case wasn't so high profiled, would it have been hard to get the amount of supporters I had? I would soon see that altruistic people are a dying breed. "Let's see who will stick with me in the long run." I said while I charged my tether.

I would wake up with my body completely drenched in sweat. The nightmares continued frequently. Many times I couldn't tell if I was awake or sleep. I was starting to mentally collapse. My mental energy was drained and I had to take my medication to calm my nerves. I was slowly becoming dependent on the meds and liquor. This traumatic experience was starting to unravel me like a ball of yarn. I still had to hold it together for my next court date which was coming up fast in a few days.

The private detective was still looking for the clerk who worked at the gas station and, to my surprise, he found him in another city. He supposedly quit his job and moved out of the city. He was scared and didn't want to be interviewed. His mother told my attorney on the phone that he didn't want anything to do with the case. He was the one person who said that there was a shootout that night. The crazy part was that he no longer worked at the gas station and moved out of the city. It was almost like the mob had scared him.

The clerk finally agreed to be interviewed by the detective the day before the court date as long as his father was there as well. We agreed, but when that time came, he flipped the script. It was a totally different ball game when the court date arrived.

"He's retracting everything he stated on the 911 tape and to the news that night," Dennis said. "He then told the police that my detective was harassing him and he wanted protection against him." Now that my detective caught up with him, he refused to testify and even made us the villains. He told the police and prosecutor that I was the only one shooting and he misstated what he saw that night.

Finally, the day came and I was back in court again. Now either I'm going against the Arabian mob or the prosecutor was playing dirty games. Once again the courtroom was filled with the Arabian guys' family and friends. This time they were twice as deep. We were outnumbered by at least 15 people. This was a nightmare. I appreciated my supporters being there to show the Judge and the media that we weren't backing down. News cameras were steadily snapping pictures of me as I came to the front with my attorney. Click! Click! Click! Click!

Dennis approached the prosecutor and the Judge for a private discussion. I could make out a little of what they were saying. It was about the clerk. The prosecutor was trying to make the judge believe that we had been harassing him into saying what we wanted to hear. It appeared that her team got to him first and was able to manipulate him into retract his statement and calling it "excited utterance," which is a statement in the heat of the moment that shouldn't be taken as sufficient proof. It was really clear to me that this prosecutor was trying everything to put me under the jail.

Of course, after the clerk flipped the script, I was outdone. Seeing how this was going nowhere but south, I was becoming restless. "What's the plan?" I asked Dennis quietly in his ear after he sat down. "If you want to put the clerk on the stand you can, but he was going to lie on you without a doubt," he said. The alternative was that if I decided not to, we could just wait to trial and put him up on the stand and cross-examine him. We can show him to be a liar that he is and put Jasmine on the stand as well. I was starting to see how Dennis was thinking.

Dennis was all about winning the war, not the battle. The Judge was planning on sending this case to a full-blown jury trial. His mind was made up after the last court date. The best strategy was to wait until it was time for trial before you showed your hand. No point in squandering your time and effort to win this battle. He wanted to focus on the war at hand. This is why he is saving Jasmine's testimony and mine for last. I agreed. I was tired of this judge anyway.

Dennis stood up and told the judge that we had no further witnesses at this time. The prosecutor looked stunned. She just knew we would bring him out and throw fuel to the fire. If he testifies against me, it would have given her more ammo to lock me up, but instead we would decide to prepare for trial.

Both parties made their final remarks and the judge bounded me over for trial. Now the pre-trial was over. This was another news sensation. "Santa shooter bounded over for trial!" Media personnel once again started snapping photos of me walking out the courtroom.

I walked out into the crowd of people outside the courtroom who couldn't even fit inside. I got really anxious and claustrophobic from the masses of people.

My barber, Sean, tapped me on my shoulder and told me to stay strong. His aunt worked for the courts and knew my attorney very well. She told him that he knows what he is doing, he's a strategist. I took a deep breath and replied, "I hope so."

As we got into the car and headed to home, all I kept thinking was, "I need a drink." The moment I stepped into the house, I raced upstairs to my closet. I opened it up and all I saw was alcohol, shoes and books. I by-passed the shoes and books and grabbed the Remy Martin bottle. My problems were manifesting themselves into an addiction. Between the anxiety medication, Remy and dejected music I was listening to, I was escaping depression. Or, at least, I thought I was.

So there I was, the shooting Santa being bonded over for trial and on house arrest. My state of mind was unstable. The slightest thing seemed to get me upset. I found myself arguing with my mom and yelling at my daughter. The pressure in the household was destroying my relationships.

My daughter had it the worst. She did not understand why her daddy was so upset and not understanding her. When I would drop her off at school, the teachers and parents who knew me would hug me and say they were praying for me. Everyone who knew me in the city knew my situation. When you are caught up in the justice system, you are not the only victim, your family is too.

"How can it get any worst for me?" I thought to myself as I sat at home one day. Suddenly, I heard a knock at the door. *"Probably a friend stopping by,"* I

guessed. I opened the door and was greeted by a middle age woman who asked if I was Marcus Weldon. "Yes. Who are you?" I asked suspiciously. "My name is Danielle and I am from Child Protective Services. Is Za'Nya home?" she asked.

"CHILD PROTECTIVE SERVICES?! Why are they here? To take my baby?" I wondered. It turned out that my daughter's mother called them on me. She heard of the shooting and saw it as an opportunity regain custody. There was also a letter in the mail with a court date on it for missed child visits.

"Mr. Weldon, you are accused of locking your daughter in the closet, and you are also accused of being the Santa Shooter. Can I come in?" What a low blow! I let her in and called my custody attorney. I wanted to know if they could take her because of my pending charges. My attorney told me that they can't use that unless you are convicted. "As far as the court date for visitation rights, well, that will be something we would have to go to court for," he explained. It was a lie, but, of course, she was trying everything to destroy my character.

Danielle from CPS asked to speak to my daughter alone. My daughter doesn't take well to strangers, especially under these circumstances. She was only 5-years-old and she too was stressed because of what was going on. Eventually, they talked and the lady came out and gave me some papers to sign. She told me that my daughter was really quiet and acting standoffish, but everything seemed ok.

I explained the situation. She heard of the shooting

on the news. This was nothing new because CPS gets false reports all the time. In fact, this was actually my third time being accused through a false CPS report. The difference in this report was that I was the Santa going around shooting people. This made it a little bit more believable that I was violent towards my baby. Once you've been painted a criminal, everything is questioned.

Now, it was time to prepare for another court date. On the same day, I literally walked from Frank Murphy Courthouse to family court. I had on the same shirt, same suit and same tie. I just stood in front of a different judge. The situation with the CPS was quickly resolved, but it added pressure to the heaviness of the already heavy burden. As my mind raced back and forth, I began to constantly mistake nightmares as reality. Imagine waking up in the middle of the night from a nightmare that felt so real that your heart pumped like you had just run a marathon!

I smelled a heavy presence of gun powder all around me. After coming so far and bouncing back from disappointment after disappointment, I was now at a crossroads once again in my life. Going through the storm is tough enough, but sitting still in an uncertain stage of idleness is even worst. Idleness allows your pessimistic imagination to run wild. I had to get control of my subconscious mind before it got full control of me.

I would watch Netflix to pass time, but Netflix was getting old. I could barely focus on books because my mind would drift and my outfits were all messed up now that I had a big tether on my leg. My boots took a beating from the big block of plastic as it laid on top of the boot, putting unwanted creases in them and sometimes rubbing the skin of my dry ankle.

House parties was another option of escaping reality, but even then I couldn't snap fully out of the depression. I put on a front for everyone, like I was doing fine, but really, I was mentally drained. Not having anything to do all day was the worst. I felt like a zombie and to avoid dumb idleness I would call people over to drink and play XBOX. Eventually the media attention died down and so did the company as everyone began to go back to their normal lives.

My new life remained the same though. I was stuck in the house with nothing to do. A once busy lifestyle was slowed down by the forces of the justice system. The roadblocks and traffic jams of life kept me from getting to any destination I felt was worthy of reaching.

My friend, Sonya, made a "Go Fund Me" account for me. It was to help keep up on my bills and legal expenses. I wasn't getting any checks while on an unpaid leave of absence from work. My girlfriend would keep me company as much as she could, but the stress of the case began to really destroy us. Arguments filled with verbal abuse went back and forth and became the norm for us. I was Santa shooting people over Mrs. Claus. I was the angry Black man that got mad because someone accidentally "bumped my girl."

So you can imagine what was going through her mind this whole time as the story circled the city. Her friends and family, no doubt, had questions about what my intentions were with this young lady and why was I out so late with a girl? Why couldn't she call her boyfriend to help her with the flat tire? These were questions that her friends probably drilled her with. Drama on drama every single night. I felt responsible for everything. I went from being the victim to the culprit on every level.

Our relationship was rocky before this situation started, but now it was an emotional roller coaster derailed by a chivalrous disaster. She stuck with me through some horrible times, but would this be the last straw? Who else was there to blame?

I couldn't fault her for thinking the way she did. She really never fully accepted the fact that I was working for a company surrounded by half-naked women in Santa suits anyway. Also, modeling brought lots of female attention, and as a 26-year-old male trying to make it to the big screen, I was only concerned about myself. I was always told by other models to write "Single" for my marital status on applications and replies in any interviews with magazine editors.

The industry wants to promote single models for marketing purposes. Your charm and charisma was everything to get opportunities, and you never wanted to close a door on an opportunity by saying that you were in a relationship. Right out of the gate, that may close certain doors for you. It's like putting yourself in a box. I thought to myself every night, *"Is this the end of my relationship, my career and my freedom?"*

Later that week, my good friend, Oscar Thomas, who was also the District 4 Manager of Detroit invited me out to Dennis Archer Jr.'s, the former mayor's son, auto show party. Oscar was another mentor of mine and was the reason I was in the political lime light in the first place. It was a private event, but I didn't really want to go, but something told me to.

I had a few hours to be out and it was an opportunity to get some fresh air and mingle a little bit. I got dressed wearing a green turtleneck and black jeans big enough to cover the tether. Hoping that no one noticed me or questioned me about the case, I tried to be as inconspicuous as possible.

As I walked into the party with Oscar, the room was full of familiar faces. It was a crowd similar to the one I'd experienced at the Brenda Jones party, the day before the incident. The room was full of round tables with white linen cloths on them. Everyone looked as if they were going to a wedding or a black tie affair. The smell of food began to circle the room as it was brought out of the kitchen.

This was the high classy crowd, the type that wouldn't pay too much attention to little ole me, right? Nope! I was wrong. A number of people approached me talking about the case. I kept my answers simple. "I'll be all right," I said mostly. But, what I had coming next was something that would leave some indelible marks on my soul and spirit. Something no one could have predicted.

As I turned to my left looking for a table to sit, I made eye contact with a Detroit police officer. We both stared at each other for a few seconds. The room went silent. Well, at least it did in my mind. This officer knew me and I knew him. In fact, he was the officer who drove me to the police station that night to be charged. But the look he gave me wasn't a bad look. It was more like a look of concern.

There was no ambiguity in his facial expression. I knew by the look in his eyes that there was something on his mind that he wanted to say to me. I approached him and asked, "Do you know who I am?" "Yes, I do," he replied calmly. I began to try to tell him my side of the story, but before I could get it out good, he cut me off and said. "I saw the gas station surveillance video tape." I was shocked. *"How is this possible? I was told that the tape didn't work,"* I said to myself.

Immediately my mind began to race and flash back to that horrible night. The feeling of that hard-plastic handle attached to my sweaty hand. I remember feeling like the trigger was biomechanically fused to my finger. I recall firing round after round after round, while wondering if the shots took effect. I heard bullets rip through the air like spitballs through a classroom. For a second it was like I was watching a movie, only I was in it. I could feel the recoil of my 40-caliber pistol as it jumped around in my hand.

The officer's reply snapped me out of it. "Oh, it does work, and from my opinion it looks like self-defense. Did you warn him first?" "Hell, yeah I did!" I exclaimed. "Well, you should tell your lawyer to get that tape."

This changed the game. If there was video footage out there, then maybe there was hope after all. "God, thank you!" I said quietly. I felt like I was dropped a lifeline from heaven like they did in the "The Hunger Games" in the heat of battle. I really needed that. There are good cops in Detroit after all.

I didn't want to be stuck in a downward spiral. I finally opened my closet and turned from the alcohol to the books. The authors I discovered included scholars such as Carter G. Woodson, Booker T. Washington, Malcolm X, and modern day thought leaders such as Malcolm Gladwell, Dr. Cornel West, Dr. Michael Eric Dyson, Michelle Alexander, Dr. Joy Degruy and Dr. Umar Abdullah-Johnson. These literary heroes became my virtual mentors.

Booker T. Washington was one of my favorites. In his book *Up from Slavery,* he talks about Black people depending on the government like a child depending on his mother. He also said something that elucidated and invalidated my theory that something was inherently wrong with me and all other Black people.

> "The influence of ancestry, however, is important in helping forward any individual or race, if too much reliance is not placed upon it. Those who constantly direct attention to the Negro youth's moral weaknesses, and compare his advancement with that of white youths, do not consider the influence of the memories which cling about the old family homesteads. I have no idea, as I have stated elsewhere, who my grandmother was. I have, or have had, uncles and aunts and cousins, but I have no

knowledge as to where most of them are."

We don't know who we are. If we knew who we were, then we'd know where we're going. Too many of us struggle with not being connected to our forefathers and now, not even being connected to the man who is our father. Dr. Joy Degruy's book, *Post Traumatic Slave Syndrome*, is a must read if you want to be part of the healing process of America's painful history. She says that we rehearse the past because the future is a mystery.

Michelle Alexander calls the prison system "the New Jim Crow." Some people tend to think that's going a little too far, but going through the process helped me understand where she was coming from. I was in school, working, serving in the community, exploring entrepreneurship and yet faced with losing it all.

In his book, *The Black Presidency*, Dr. Michael Eric Dyson says the reason it's hard to talk about racism and structures of racism is because we are in the "age of Obama". His theory was that the Age of Obama made it easy to forget the poor Black and Brown people because, now that we have outliers like Oprah and Obama, the playing fields now seem equal.

It is true that we as African Americans have come a long way, but as Malcolm X said, "If you stick a knife in my back nine inches and pull it out six inches, there's no progress. If you pull it all the way out that's not progress. Progress is healing the wound that the blow made."

My reading and interests in books became more eclectic over time. I began to pick up books like *Black Man with a Gun Reloaded* by Reverend Kenn Blanchard,

Negros with Guns by Robert F. Williams, *The School Revolution* by Ron Paul and *The Arc of Justice* by Kevin Boyle. I began to study the Constitution, the Bill of Rights and breaking down the structure of the government.

After reading so much from these various authors, I was inspired and decided to write my story. It was another way for me to have an outlet and keep myself from going insane as the news and social media continued to tell their version of my truth. I had to look in the mirror and ask, "What am I doing to create change?"

CHAPTER 9
How Did I Get Here?

"Too many young folk have addiction to superficial things and not enough conviction for substantial things like justice, truth and love."

– Dr. Cornel West

After high school, your environment changes and, if you're not careful, your mind could stay the same. Understand that now you have to go make a living. "Welcome to the real world!" I used to say. It's about you doing better in your life at this point. Are you working? Are you in college? You are no longer in competition for the attention of the classroom, but instead the attention of the world.

Most young black males look at having nice things as a grade for success. Who's got the nicest car? Are you wearing name-brand clothes? It's more about looking successful than actually being successful. I was a part-time student, and I remember when I first got hired at the casino working for the housekeeping department. I felt like I had it made.

Before that, I was taking my money and investing in liabilities and not assets. Stuff like getting rims on my car and having the latest stuff. I had a 2006 Dodge Magnum that I painted candy red. Everybody called it the "Jolly Rancher". I put Lamborghini doors, 24-inch rims and mad sounds in it too. By far, I had the hottest Dodge Magnum on the eastside of Detroit. Everyone wanted to ride with me downtown and ride to Belle Isle. We called it "stuntin", which meant showing off your nice car to the "have not's of the Detroit."

We would go through all the hoods riding back to back. I had the Magnum. My homie, Rell, had the Challenger. My boy, Wyman, had a Range Rover. A few of my other friends had nice cars too. We put so much Armor-All on our tires that they shined like fresh, hot tar. The rims would be so clean that you could see your reflection in them!

Being a new father, my mind was always thinking about two people, and I couldn't afford to get caught up in the dangerous streets anymore. Every week we would argue about changing our routine. I wanted a change of scenery and to try new things and start playing it safe, but Wyman had no problem hitting the local neighbor bar at any time of night. Wyman was more of a brother to me, and he could often convince me to do anything.

"Yoooo, Marcus! Let's hit downtown and look for some hoes!" Wyman said. "I'm with it bro!" I said excitedly. It became normal to call women disrespectful names without even noticing it. It was how we talked in the hood.

The sound of the high-powered motors made the streets shake as we flew up and down the highway, showing off our toys. "This shit is going to be crazy!" we would say, laughing. Just the thought of the ladies smiling at us because of our souped-up vehicles made us feel good. We loved the attention that these cars gave us. It took a while before I started to question this twisted, superficial addiction we had.

At that time, I was also managing a rap group. We called ourselves "DMW" *Detroit's Most Wanted.* Funny, I know. The hip hop music game was the hot thing to do. Detroit was inspired by "Big Sean" who I went to high school with. Watching him become who he is today up close was definitely inspiration. It was the feeling that we could make it in the rap game, too.

We were trying to fit this big money, hard core image to sell mixtapes. My artists were Arsenal Showtyme and Meech. We would show off at clubs and have our songs played in the clubs. Of course, the girls were always trying to holla' at us! They loved nice cars in Detroit because it meant money, and usually drug money.

Quite the opposite, everyone I hung around for the most part had jobs or legal hustles. We all kept it legit. Of course, the masses of people we were "stuntin' on" thought otherwise. We were making unintentional enemies because of all the attention we were getting. People who didn't have nice cars hated us when we came down the block. At the time, I couldn't figure out why. I felt it was simple: Work hard and get what you wanted. But it didn't work like that in "The D." People work hard to take what you have. Some people are extremely jealous in Detroit.

Stuff got rough for us. We got into fights in the clubs. I even got my Cartier glasses taken one night. After a while, our lives started to take different paths. I was slowly getting out of the "partying and hanging out late" mode and getting more into entrepreneurship. But for some reason, Wyman couldn't let go of the late-night hanging and partying every weekend.

To tell the truth, if it wasn't for my daughter and my goals, I would have probably ended up dead or in jail a long time ago. I would have probably killed that guy who took my glasses that night. The toughest guys in the streets were the ones who had nothing to lose. The unexpected freedom that comes with having nothing to lose can be scary. Except that wasn't me. I was in the middle of an intense custody battle for my daughter. I had someone to lose. In fact, I had a lot to lose.

The custody battle started when my relationship went sour. I felt like I was a pawn in a chess game with my daughter's mother. Even worse, after years of trusting my best friend, "White Boi," I learned a hard lesson on friendship. When my daughter was born I found out that White Boi started sleeping with my girlfriend. The information came from a surprising, very unexpected source.

White Boi's girlfriend saw me at a club and told me everything. "You better get that bitch!" she said. "I'm tired of him, and I'm no longer keeping secrets. Yo' friend ain't shit and your baby mama is a joke!" This actually shouldn't have come as a surprise because I saw the signs, but I guess I was in denial.

I was hurt and angry, and in response to how she

was feeling, White Boi's girlfriend tried to make a move on me. She was drunk and emotionally torn and wanted revenge. I couldn't do it, even out of spite, so I turned her down. This was the rise and fall of my already rocky relationship with my baby's mama.

You see, I did my dirt too, and I saw signs that she wasn't the one for me, but when a baby comes into play, it's almost like you've got to make it work. The child support system was killing me, and I saw firsthand how that system can break fathers – even the good fathers. It's a broken system just like the criminal justice system. But, to make a long story short, I had to cut off two important relationships in my life. My custody battle began as backlash of resentment and childish games manifested themselves. A chaotic lifestyle was what I was getting used to.

I was still really trying to find myself, but I didn't know how or where to start. The hot thing to do was to get in the music game. However, that was beginning to get watered down by the masses of Black, urban kids flooding the streets with the same-sounding gangster rap. I had the mindset to become successful. I just needed guidance and some exposure to new things to regain the curiosity I once had when I was younger.

When I was younger, I was trying to connect the dots. In order to do that, you need to become what Malcolm Gladwell calls an "Outlier". You have to be "set apart from the common paradigm" that many young, Black males get caught up in. The question is: How do you become an "Outlier"?

Becoming an outlier has a lot to do with your environment, experiences, where you were born and even the era in which you were born. There are pools of information you draw from via books and even classes you take. Your environment molds you, but everyone doesn't have the same open mindset to break out of their harsh reality.

The most important part in determining if you will become an "Outlier" is your "Cultural Legacy." Hard work, morals and rigorous thinking are deeply rooted in cultural legacies. "It makes a difference where and when we grew up. The culture we belong to and the legacies passed down by our forebears shape the patterns of our achievements in ways we cannot begin to imagine," Gladwell says.

Most of the people I grew up with have stayed in the same environment and do the same thing over and over. They never try anything new or leave the Detroit city limits. Limited experiences in life will cause limited creativity, which will hinder your ability to think outside the box for new ideas. This could cause you to stay in that same "hood mentality" as they call it in Detroit.

By experiencing urban and suburban school schools, I was well rounded. I could blend in both areas. I could hold my own in Detroit. Learning from my mistakes as a sheep, I was able to put on wolves' clothing, when needed, to survive. I could communicate and relate to those in the suburban communities as well.

I experienced a "culture shock" early on in my life. At Avondale, I had to mingle and mix with different cultures. I had to learn how to walk and talk with a diverse group of people. I couldn't bring that same "Detroit Swag" to the suburban areas because it would be intimidating to people. This ended up helping me in the future.

Eventually I got back in school and made the transition from housekeeping to the engineering department. I doubled my income in a year and improved my resume. In a blue collar city like Detroit, it was important for me to learn to work with my hands. The skilled trades and engineering jobs were wide open in the city, easily making up to six-figure salaries per year. Lots of young people were taking advantage of the opportunities they had in front of them, including me.

Seeing my potential and eagerness to learn, my older cousin decided to take me under his wing as his mentee. I now had multiple mentors; my parents, my pastor and my cousin. This was a huge blessing since so many Black boys don't have even one positive role model or mentor in their life.

My cousin, Ted, introduced me to another business mindset and new way of thinking. He was older than me, but we shared similar paths and experiences. He opened my eyes to other ways to make money and think outside the box. "You don't have to be involved in the entertainment business to be successful," he informed me. Unfortunately, too many African-American boys think that the only way out of the hood is through the music industry, throwing parties, dealing drugs, or becoming an athlete.

This is because there are not enough successful people to look up to that we can actually talk to. Can you imagine having a doctor in your family, or a successful, high-profile lawyer? To be able to pick their brains on how they became successful would be a gift in itself.

I had to stop and think. Are the people in the urban Detroit area that lazy and don't want to better themselves? My opinion from my experiences is that it's a relationship between effort and reward. Some people are non-productive when the work that they are being asked to do isn't meaningful or is poorly suited to help them meet their basic needs.

People who could actually see the relationship between the effort and reward would work harder because they see the light at the end of the tunnel. It helps when you see the value in your task. This is why the vocational programs are important, and we need to bring them back to every Detroit Public School along with real Black History classes. The trade industry is in desperate need of electricians, carpenters, HVAC workers and plumbers, too.

College isn't always the answer for everyone. We need options. History class would be more meaningful with more discussion of the black experience and learning trades could help you make money right after high school. That's important, right?

"So what did 'Big Cuz' have in mind?" I wondered. *"What else could I do? What other industries are tangible for the poor or middle-class families?"* I had a meeting with him and the plan he had wasn't anything I would have thought. "This might sound crazy," he said, "But, I got a patent on a weighted dog vest." He stated that forty-four percent of Americans own dogs and over half of them are obese because of neglect.

A busy dog owner can't give the attention that his or her pet needs. So, because of the neglected exercise, the dogs have a lot of built up anxiety and energy. You're supposed to walk your dog thirty minutes a day, but, of course, most families are too busy. With the vest we can cut that walking time in half!

I totally got the concept as soon as he said it. My family had owned dogs forever, and my dad learned how to train them through K-9 Safety Consultants. They were, and still are, the best of the best. So understanding the pet world was easy for me.

He had it all planned out. He went to China and got it manufactured. I networked with stores and potential investors. It was a grind! We would go from city to city promoting the product. We would meet celebrities like Dame Dash, one of the founders of Roca Fella records, and Dolvett Quince, a celebrity trainer on *NBC's the Biggest Loser*, along with all kinds of professional athletes and pitched the product to them.

My first important business meeting was with Clark Durant, the co-founder and former CEO of the Cornerstone Schools, where I'd attended during my elementary and middle school years. Durant was a Republican politician in the state of Michigan, and a candidate for the U. S. Senate in 2012. The meeting took place at the Detroit Athletic Club. I was not prepared for what I was about to experience.

As we pulled, up the valet parking lot was full of Mercedes Benz and Range Rovers. Everybody was wearing suits and looking like businessmen. This was real money! I was not ready for this. My suit was too big and I didn't know proper meeting etiquette at all. I slouched in my chair and I was extremely nervous. So nervous that I couldn't even drink my tea correctly. I was shaking. I mean, think about it: If you've never sat in a business meeting with white men in suits, it can be really intimidating.

Ted, his business partner, Caleb, and I walked in to meet Mr. Durant. Mr. Durant was rushing. He told everybody to turn their phones off. He only had a few minutes so we had to quickly make our point. I was the one who set the meeting up, and there I was feeling inferior to someone of his stature. As a result, I don't think he took us seriously.

The meeting was a disaster and we did not come away with any investment. But the points I took away from that experience were priceless and helped me to understand the power of networking and building relationships. Even if you're not on someone's level, you can learn how to connect with them and handle your business.

I learned so much from traveling with Ted. My mind was expanding, and I lost that fear of stepping out on faith and trying something new. Of course, people laughed at the idea that I was selling dog products. This isn't the ideal hustle for a twenty-three-year-old. But the biggest experience was yet to come.

After brainstorming, we added more features to it. We made it convert into a life jacket (once you pull the weights out, of course). It was like a family business. We wanted to have something that we could hand down to our kids. Building generational wealth could not only change our circumstances, but the circumstances of our city. I had to pass down this mentorship that I was blessed to have. It was in me to change lives.

One day we got word that there was a *Shark Tank* audition in Chicago. *Shark Tank* is the TV show on ABC that has three or four business investors (called 'Sharks'). They listen to pitches from entrepreneurs seeking funding for their business, products, or services. Ted and I hit the road for the audition.

The producers loved it and after a few interviews and background checks, the next step was to record our pitch and send it off to them. Except something came back on the background check. Ted and I owed back taxes on a house that he sold me a few years back. Both of our names were appearing on the house. With outstanding taxes owed, one of us would have to take ownership of this debt and, in doing so, not appear on the show.

So, I took the blame for the debt. Ted was the CEO of the company and was the reason I even had this opportunity. It was about the bigger picture, which was going on the show, getting a deal and some major exposure. Of course, it was heartbreaking, but I was focused on the end result.

After sending the pitch, Ted and Caleb were flown to California. Regardless of the background check, I went anyway at my own expense. To me, this was about seeing things through and getting the gold. Down in California we met other *Shark Tank* contestants. Two of them were sisters, Ashley Jung & Paige Dellavalle, with whom we later became friends.

"If we get a deal, we will tattoo the logo of our company on our legs," Ashley said, with a credulous look on her face. Paige agreed. We promised to celebrate with them if they got the deal. The next morning was their big day, and they were confident.

Ashley and Paige's company is Stella Valle. It is "a jewelry brand that inspires confidence and who you are and where you are going." The two girls were slim and built like Victoria's Secret models, with perfectly straight teeth. Their personalities put me in the mindset of the Kardashians, but they had an edge to them because they were army brats.

"Cousin Marcuuuusss!" is what they would call me. They always reminded me of how blessed and lucky I was to experience such a great opportunity at such a young age. I was blessed to have had mentors that paved ways to experiences that I probably never would have encountered if I hadn't joined my cousin on this incredible project.

I realize that it is not common for young Black men to be in Los Angeles getting ready for a Shark Tank audition. Just a few weeks before this, I was a Detroiter, wearing Cartier glasses, going to clubs and hanging out in the hood. My mind was on one thing: stuntin' and getting hoes. But, now, because of Ted, I was about to be part of history. If LaGuard gets a deal, we could be millionaires.

The next day we learned that the two girls got the deal. We held up our end of the bargain and took them out for drinks. The two girls chickened out on the tattoos of course, but it was all fun, and I was excited to see them succeed.

The sisters were Shark Tank survivors who partnered with Lori Greiner & Mark Cuban. Unfortunately, we didn't have the results that we were looking for. When I got home fresh off my flight I was tired and devastated. We jumped through hoops to get Ted on the show. I just knew that LaGuard was ready for a deal. We needed to do more to get their attention.

I woke up the next morning with that horrible, empty feeling. I had to snap out of it and let it roll off. I swallowed my pride and got dressed for work that morning ready to fake my way throughout the day. I was acting like I was happy, but I was really down. Anyhow, what I had coming next would be the straw that broke the camel's back.

As I walked in the building everyone was discussing a carjacking that happened on the eastside of Detroit on Chalmers and Harper at a Coney Island last night. It was all on the news that morning. A dark colored Range Rover was stolen and the driver was fatally shot. I was so caught up in my life problems that I didn't even think twice about the carjacking.

Without warning, my phone began to blow off the hook. It was my boy, Chris. "Now, what could he want so bad at this time in the morning? He knows I'm at work!" I said to myself. I answered the phone to crying and screaming. The deadly carjacking that left one person dead was my boy, Wyman. He was carjacked and killed around the time I went to bed upset.

I dropped the phone and collapsed on the floor. I was struck hard by this one. I cried like a teething two-year-old. It felt like the life was zapped out of me completely. There was nothing anyone could say to pull me off that ground. I eventually had to leave work. I couldn't work under that stress. I raced to Wyman's father's house to get the full story.

It turned out that Wyman was out late at a Coney Island, meeting some girls and two guys robbed him and carjacked him. Some jealous punks from the neighborhood. The passenger he was with got away, but Wyman died in the parking lot.

This was a turning point in my life. The first time you lose someone close to you because they were murdered changes your life. At that moment, I realized that if I was going to ride in nice cars, I was seriously going to have to change my scenery and get my CPL. These streets were too dangerous and I was cutting it too close.

The death of a close friend was an experience that most African-Americans had. "Black on Black crime" or "proximity crime" was the norm. That experience, along with the countless numbers of break-ins and violent encounters I had with my own people, would make anyone question their cultural pride.

I witnessed the most jealously from my people. I'd witnessed my church and my Pastor's properties get broken into by my own people. My church did a lot for the community, but, time and time again, it was set back and destroyed by my own people. At that point what made me different from any other white person who felt this way? I, too, felt that my race was a problem.

Later, after the guys were caught and charged, they were sentenced to 15 years in prison. One of them was bipolar and was able to avoid life in prison because of the mental disorder. Another lesson I learned was that mental disorders are a heavy problem in America; especially in the poor, urban areas.

The lack of money comes with the lack of health care. Also, a lot of Black people I know refuse to get regular checkups and are in denial of mental health issues. As Tom Burrell writes in his book, *Brainwashed*, "REPRESSION OF DEPRESSION: Denial of and inability to cope with depression and mental health issues. Shaming and blaming individuals who try to get help. Undiagnosed mental health issues exacerbate problems and often lead to incarceration." This was a prime example in my life.

All I kept thinking was, "If Wyman had a gun, he would be alive today." America has an extreme mental illness problem that isn't on the priority list of most politicians. Research has shown that America is number one in incarceration and also number one in mental illness disorders. More than half of all prisoners have mental illness and should be in a position to get treatment. Instead, states are closing down mental health clinics and opening more prisons. With the government operating backwards, how do we put our trust in them? The police response was horrible the night of Wyman's death.

According to American Police Beat, the average

response time for an emergency call is 10 minutes. Atlanta has one of the worst response times of 11 to 12 minutes, and Nashville comes in at 9 minutes. Detroit, on the other hand, takes the cake. One figure put Detroit's pre-bankruptcy police response times for high-priority crimes at a staggering 58 minutes! Kevyn Orr, the former Emergency Manager of Detroit, used this figure, in part, to justify recommending Detroit filing for bankruptcy. I refused to put my faith in Detroit police. Self-protection is better than no protection.

Things got worst with the back and forth with my baby-mama drama. I had won my custody case. I was ready to move on with my life and just take care of my daughter. However, my ex-girlfriend couldn't take rejection. So she did the unthinkable. She left the state with my daughter and filed a false Child Protective Services (CPS) complaint on me. But not just any CPS complaint – a sexual assault complaint.

Can you imagine a Child Protective Service worker coming to your door stating that you need to come to the CPS building for questioning? Can you imagine a team of CPS workers going through your house searching for evidence to an accusation that wasn't even true? This went on for three whole months. I didn't see or talk to my baby during that entire time, and I was losing sleep wondering whether or not she was alright. What if someone else did something to her and my ex was trying to blame me for it? This had happened before in other situations, but the cases were dismissed.

With all of this hitting me at once back to back it

had to be the lowest moment of my life without a doubt. Why were things going this way for me? What was God getting me prepared for? I was a big Malcolm Gladwell reader and his newest book at that time was *David and Goliath: Underdogs, Misfits, and The Art of Battling Giants*. The story was delivered in a way that made me think deeper into the story.

David was the underdog, but was prepared to fight Goliath the whole time. He was excellent with his sling shot; and he was actually celebrated in the Bible for killing off bears and lions to protect his sheep. Can you imagine being faced with a bear or lion attacking your sheep? Your slingshot can throw one rock at a time and if you miss or wound that animal it would become a more dangerous situation.

I've heard someone say that there is nothing more dangerous than a wounded animal. Those instincts kick in and it's over! You've got to have precise accuracy and God on your side, and David did. Those lions and bears prepared David for the biggest test of his life… Goliath! So, I had to wonder what were the lions and bears in my life preparing me for? What or who was my Goliath?

So, the battles I'd had finding myself and figuring out who I was, getting in trouble as a teenager, transitioning to a completely different environment, and my custody case were all my little obstacles that were making me tougher for this giant trial. This trial was heavy on my mind. I didn't know where I was going to be in the future. I could lose everything. I didn't know where I was going to lay my head after this. "How did I get here?" I asked myself over and over again.

The closer it got to my trial, the deeper the pain felt. The anxiety I was feeling was real. You could easily go crazy with everything that was going on. There were three or four people I knew who were going through the justice system at the same time. Were we all going to end up in jail? With all of this on my mind, I was unable to think straight. I was always looking for something to take the pain away.

After giving up the alcohol, I started smoking cigarettes. I was on the back porch one day, and my daughter found me smoking some cigarettes I had taken out of my brother's car. She said, "Ooooo, you smoking!" "Girl, get outta here!" I yelled. My daughter is a tattle-tale!

The truth was, I was embarrassed that she saw me filling my lungs and brain with over 4,000 chemicals like nicotine, tar, and carbon monoxide, as well as formaldehyde, ammonia, hydrogen cyanide, arsenic, and DDT. I had to get my act together. My life was too messy. Why was I always learning lessons the hard way?

The problem in that moment was that I needed something to calm my nerves before I opened my laptop and inserted the surveillance video from the gas station the night of the shooting. My attorney finally got a copy of the video after I called him and told him about my little encounter I had with police officer.

We had to take the recording to a video forensic expert to be unencrypted. Kent, the video expert, told us when he got it, "… the video seemed to be intentionally encrypted and missing pieces and was hard to open." Finally, the day came for me to watch his version of the recording to see if everything actually happened like I thought it happened.

My hand was shaking like I had Parkinson's disease when I pressed play. As the video played, I relived the pain of the traumatic shooting. I was about to witness myself, Marcus Weldon, in a Santa Claus suit, shoot two people on film for the first time since the day the shooting took place on December 21, 2014. This video had the power to incriminate me or exonerate me!

I watched the video with baited breath. I could see the Arabian man go to his car and turn around. I could see my arm pointed in his direction. Then, I saw something that I knew had happened, but couldn't prove it up until this point. I sat back and thought, "This one piece of evidence could save my ass!"

CHAPTER 10

I Actually Learned Something in School

"Sorrows are our best educator. A man can see further through a tear than a telescope."

– Bruce Lee

I was broken, my life was spiraling down and didn't seem to be slowing up. My trial date was moved several times from January to March 21st and then it was pushed to May and finally to June 13, 2016. The closer it got to the trial date, the more emotional I became. I tried to be positive and use other things to keep my attention, but I kept rehearsing bad memories like what happened with my friend, Wyman.

After Wyman's death, I started hating my own people. "Why were Blacks killing Blacks? Why were we acting like savages?" I asked myself over and over again. I had no intentions at this point to fight for social justice. In fact, I didn't want to be associated with my city anymore.

As I reflected on my actions as teenager, were they the actions of a thug or the actions of person succumbing and adapting to his environment? How much more developed would my mentality have been if I had grown up away from the harsh reality of urban Detroit? Or would it have mattered at all? One can only speculate. This is when my pastor became very important in my life.

Pastor Alonzo Bell re-educated me on Black history. He taught me about the reality of concepts like "white flight" and gentrification. Pastor Bell opened my eyes to the intentional neglect of urban schools and projects. I learned to think deeply about poverty and slavery. I learned to observe the real-life effects of the two.

Two of my favorite authors spoke of these things often. To my surprise, both Dr. Cornel West and Dr. Michael Eric Dyson were coming to Detroit on the same weekend in February! I had to make sure that I met both of them.

I decided to write them each a letter and prayed that I would be able to deliver them face-to-face. In the letters, I wanted to briefly tell them my story. I wanted to express how they inspired me, a bit of my background and see if there was anything they could do to help me. I would take anything from either of them – advice, support, or even acknowledgement of my situation through their social media channels.

The event with Dr. Cornel West was amazing! A dinner was included with the purchase of my ticket. I wore a dark blue suit, a red, white and blue checkered tie to offset the white dress shirt and black dress shoes. Everything was tailor fit and well put together, if I may say so myself.

This event included all kinds of high-profile people. From television news anchor, Huel Perkins, to City Councilwoman Mary Sheffield. Then, there was Dr. Cornel West himself. He was dressed in a black and white suit like the honorable Dr. Martin Luther King, Jr. He looked just like he did on television—scholarly glasses along with his puffy, Frederick Douglas hair.

The crowd responded with enthusiasm and energy as he gave his powerful speech on race, mass incarnation and inequality among the poor and working-class people. The standing ovations as he spoke echoed throughout the building. The Flint Water Crisis was a hot topic, as young and old, rich and poor, black and white, kids and adults drank water poisoned with lead and other contaminants for two years, under negligent Emergency Management.

As I sat at my table and ate my food, I spoke with people around the table about the Flint Water Crisis. They were pleased to hear a young man so passionate about helping others. The lady next to me told me that l had a bright future ahead of me. She obviously didn't see that big block of plastic, I brought along with me on my right leg that I kept tucked underneath my chair.

That box always reminded me that my future was uncertain. Every time I would get excited about my goals and dreams, that black, home imprisonment system reminded me of my once-a-week responsibility to check in at a local jail with a tether officer. As the night ended it was my time to navigate through the crowd like twelve-year-old at a carnival making his way to the front of the line. Only the rollercoaster was not a physical one.

Instead, I was making my way through the crowd on a mental rollercoaster of emotions. This was the opportunity to meet a man whom I'd looked up to; and now I had the chance to hand deliver a letter that could have easily been lost in his pile of junk mail if I would have just emailed to him.

When I finally got to the front, I shook his hand with confidence and delivered my message. His eyes got wide as I told him a brief summary of what happened. "I'll definitely read it brother," he said, as his puffy hair brushed against my face when he leaned in for a hug. That was cool. Meeting him, that is. Not so much the puffy hair on my face!

At the event with Dr. Michael Eric Dyson, there was a panel discussion and a question and answer period with an open mic. I decided to get out of my comfort zone and go to the mic. I shared a bit of my thoughts on the state of the black community from my perspective. People started clapping. I thought, *"Maybe I can do this public speaking thing!"* Dr. Dyson said, "That's a good point, brother!" I was able to get a picture with him when it was over.

Afterward a candidate for a judicial seat approached me and said, "What you said is good. You've got a story." I didn't tell her exactly what I was going through, but she could tell I was into something.

"Who's your attorney?" she asked curiously. I gave her his name. She said, "Oh yeah, he's good. He has a lot of cases so he may seem bombarded, but that's because he's good." I felt some sense of relief because she was confirming what I had already heard from many other trusted sources.

I had reached out to so many people, but it was hard to tell who was really with me. I'd also met Dr. Umar

Johnson, a Pan-Africanist, Black civil rights activist. He had become really popular, drawing large crowds when he speaks. He is even trying to fund an all-black, African college.

To meet Dr. Johnson, I drove over an hour to get to Flint, Michigan, where he was speaking. The struggle for me to get here was unbelievable. Not only did I get hungry in a city where the water was unsafe, I got lost. Then, when I finally got there, my tether began to die of low battery! I quickly plugged my leg into an outlet nearby as people walked past looking at my ankle jewelry plugged into the wall like a cell phone.

Dr. Johnson was wearing a dark navy-blue suit with a gold tie. He was about 6'3" and 230 lbs. His dark skin and full beard reminded me of the rapper, Rick Ross, but his passionate message made him sound like the late Marcus Garvey.

As I approached Dr. Johnson after his speech, I watched his demeanor and those around him. The people of Flint were hurting. They felt that America had forsaken them. One thing that touched my soul was watching this young, black girl wearing a blue top and brown jeans. She looked as if she was about the age of 12 and she was fighting her way through the crowd to get to the speaker. This reminded me of the story in the Bible of the woman fighting through the crowd to get to Jesus in St. Mark 5:27.

The young girl was in tears, screaming, "They're trying to kill us! They're trying to kill us!" I assumed she was referring to the government. She was looking for hope and felt he was the answer. She looked at him like he was a modern-day Moses who came to save the Hebrew people from bondage. Only this wasn't Egypt. It was Flint, Michigan, an American city with a poisoned water system.

When she finally got to him. He stopped what he was doing and hugged the girl for about 30 seconds straight. The flashes from cameras all over the room did their best to capture this touching moment. This put things in perspective for me and probably many others in the world. So many broken, black families are obliviously looking for a leader; someone they can trust. They are looking for a Moses-like figure.

I met him face-to-face after his speech. He gave me a concerned look as I told him what was happening to me. "I mean, it's like a bad dream," I said, as he wrote his phone number along with an autograph on his book. He told me to keep him updated on this matter. "Will do!" I responded excitedly.

He gave me his personal number so I called him. We set up times to talk, but he often didn't answer. So, I stopped calling him. This is when I started questioning, *"Who is really in this to help me?"* I didn't know who was in it for the cause, who was in it for themselves or who was in it to really help me. I felt as if I was being spun around like a hula hoop during this frantic state of uncertainty. All I really needed from any of the leaders was a simple conversation of invigoration.

Now, I knew that they were very busy individuals with thousands of people trying to contact them, so I tried not to get into my feelings too much. Nevertheless, I felt my case hit on some major tension points and intertwined with what's going on in the world today.

I learned a lot from those brothers. Your word is your bond and if you promise to contact someone, you should do it. I had hoped to get more support from them. Finally, after not hearing from three of the men I looked up to so much, I decided I would try something that was completely foreign to me: The National Rifle Association.

Rick Ector invited me to go with him to the Michigan State Capitol in Lansing, Michigan to an NRA rally. I looked at the flyer on their website that described it as a 2nd Amendment March. They had State Representatives, Senators and other folks as speakers. I called a friend and asked him about it and he told me to be careful and not to get in trouble. "I'll be cool," I told him.

I needed to do some investigating to prepare for the 2nd Amendment March. What should I expect? This was foreign to me. It wasn't that I'd never experienced any type of "cultural shock". By me working and going to school in the suburbs, I had friends that were all kinds of colors: Caucasian, Latino, and even Indian. Some of my good friends were Caucasian and were very supportive of me during this time of need. Some of them wrote me my best character letters and even sent me money for court.

During that time, I was even contacted by a one of the V.I.P. at my job (who was Caucasian) who emailed me a letter of encouragement. But I never received a phone call or email from my mentor (who was Black) who was also was a V.I.P at my job. Both were in high power positions and maybe had a lot to lose in contacting me. But the one who stood up and encouraged me was not the one who I expected to do so.

Taking all of this into account, I was prepared to step outside of my comfort zone and attend the march. I looked up every speaker that would take the stage that day. One of them stood out to me C.J Grisham. I really hoped to meet him.

It was a little cold, so I wore a fitted, wool plaid jacket with a matching hat, camouflage pants and matching shoes with a 2nd amendment shirt on. I guess you can say I was trying to fit the stereotype of what I thought white, country gun owners looked like. I also wanted to be myself and show my urban characteristics.

The drive to Lansing was an hour and a half long. When I arrived, it was a sight to see! Men belonging to the Militia wore army camouflage uniforms, AR-15 on their backs and 45-caliber pistols on their hips with dark shades over their eyes. I would be a liar if I said I wasn't intimidated by the weapons and the color of their skin. But I also would be a liar if I told you that the majority of them that I came in contact with were not friendly.

There were some who were standoffish and didn't seem to want to be bothered with my conversation. It didn't bother me though. Truth is, I've experienced this before. Some whites have never come in contact with Black people before. You can tell the ones who have experienced urban America and the ones who haven't right away. The images they see on television and what they were told about us is what they go by.

There were over 200 people in attendance. Some of the speakers were senators and state representatives dressed in suits. The majority of the crowd was white, but the few blacks who were there, I knew personally. Rick Ector introduced me to some of the attendees, and since he was well respected, I was given the same respect. Many of them remembered my case on the news and wanted to hear my story.

As each speaker took the stage delivering a powerful pro-gun speech, vendors of the NRA and other gun groups began to sell their merchandise. I walked around networking and shaking hands with the right people showing confidence and sincerity. I ran to each speaker as they walked off stage giving them a letter similar to the ones I gave to Dr. Dyson and Dr. West, until I finally ran into C.J Grisham.

During this time of racial tension between police officers, white supremacy groups, and Black Nationalists in constant beef, it is easy to side with your own people and shun other cultures—even the ones who are good. I, too, have been guilty of this, but was now experiencing what is called "Cognitive Dissonance". "Anxiety that results from simultaneously holding contradictory or otherwise incompatible attitudes, beliefs, or the like, as when one likes a person but disapproves strongly of one of his or her habits," Dr. Joy DeGruy explains in her book.

Because of my situation, I was often angry with all Arabian people and hated all police officers. Then, I had moments of compassion for those who had nothing to do with my situation. Everyday my beliefs were challenged.

It was finally time for the main speaker, C.J. Grisham, from Texas. He was an advocate for the "open carry" law that allows weapons to be carried publicly versus being concealed. Grisham had a high-profile case that he has been speaking about all over the country. I wrote a letter to him, and one of the Michigan State Representatives, similar to the ones I'd written before and included an excerpt from my manuscript. I brought it with me to the rally.

When some people found out who I was, they asked me if I wanted to go on stage and talk about it. I was still waiting to go to trial so I didn't want to get up in front of people and say anything! Others were looking at me kind of weird, but after I started speaking and sounded articulate, I was welcomed into different groups.

After he finished speaking, I got a chance to meet C.J., who was about 5'6" tall and wearing a light green jacket, brown cargo pants and a big revolver attached to his hip like the Western movies. He had a very friendly demeanor and was quite attentive as I to what I had to say. C.J. was quite an impressive, retired U.S. Army First Sergeant and military blogger. His profile was on Wikipedia and it said he was a soldier in the counterintelligence military occupational specialty field and a combat veteran of the Iraq War and War in Afghanistan. I reached out to him through Facebook. He called me three days later.

He Googled me, found out I was legit and promoted my case on his social media sites. He had like 20,000 followers. Through his site, somebody from Texas actually sent one hundred dollars to my GoFundMe account that I used to help cover my legal fees and other expenses. I had a long talk with Grisham and he explained that he was trying to bring Black people and white people together on the gun issue. "It's nothing to do with race. It's about the right to defend yourself," he said.

After speaking further, C.J. agreed to help me get more funding, too. "Honestly," I told him, "I think a lot of people are afraid to jump and back me up because it has me as the shooter and not the one being shot. It doesn't have the same appeal as Trayvon Martin because I am the one shooting."

At the thought of this, I was kind of upset. I mean, don't all Black lives matter? Not just those who have lost their lives, but also those who are innocent, but assumed guilty. Even C.J. and other folks that I met had to get to know me first before believing I was "okay". There are a lot of white people who have not come in contact with Black people at any point in their lives. As a result, the images they see on TV is what they judge us on as a people.

At this point, I wasn't turning down any help. C.J. counseled me on how to prepare if the video from my case went viral. He said I would get a lot of media attention. It could bring a lot of things to me. The nightmares will continue. I might get jumpy thinking people are coming around me. The video will play over and over and people will have their own opinions on it and all of this could be going on while I was sitting in jail. I mean, even though I had a strong case, my lawyer told me I was still facing 15 years in prison!

All of this helped me to understand that I actually learned something in school. I learned how to build relationships with new people. I learned how to do research. I learned how to ask for help. I learned how not to give up when things don't go your way the first time. You need all of this when you're going through a tough situation that seems impossible. Through my rough times, I found that there is redemption even in pain, ruin and heartbreak.

I did some research on the NRA to see how it was founded. Reverend Kenn Blanchard gave a very detailed breakdown of the gun group and its history. Robert F. Williams's story was very interesting to me.

Robert Franklin Williams was a Civil Rights leader and author. In the 1950s and early 1960s, he was president of the Monroe, North Carolina chapter of the National Association for the Advancement of Colored People (NAACP). I read on Wikipedia that he was big on self-defense for African Americans in the United States. He also was a member of the NRA and created a group called the Black Guard. This was a piece of history that missed the books!

Other groups like the Black Panthers and African-American Muslim groups were heavily influenced by William's pro-gun movement. Through my new reading materials, I was finding all kinds of heroes, and I needed them.

The journey through the criminal justice system is very mentally, physically and spiritually draining, not just on the one experiencing it, but on their family also. This is what I call the "Trilateral Wear Down." I found myself in unfamiliar territory. I was thrown off my square and praying for a way out. What I've learned through this process is that it helps to have a routine in place. I decided to start writing while my future was uncertain, so I could share my raw emotions – the ups and downs.

I've gotten together a routine that has helped me get through so far. If you are caught up and in the system like me, let me give you some advice and break down this system for you. You need to exercise every part of your body and conserve your whole self.

First, you need to exercise your body. Your physical exhaustion is part of the plan to win their case against you. It's like a boxing match, the one who tires out first is the one who usually loses the fight. Exercising your physical muscles does more for you than you may think. Regular exercise can increase self-confidence, it can relax you, and it can lower the symptoms associated with mild depression and anxiety, which you may encounter like I have.

Exercise can also improve your sleep, which is often disrupted by stress. You also have to eat right, which is part of reducing stress. Go to the gym regularly, especially when you are down. The court will be looking for you to lose weight, look sickly and terrified. In jail, it will be extremely hard for you to stay encouraged, especially if you cannot afford your bond. Not knowing what the hell is going on out there is rough. The more it wears on you, the more likely you will probably take a plea deal for something that you possibly didn't do.

I stepped up my gym routine big time while I was

on house arrest. I got a pull up bar and a weight belt. It was part of my personal, self-defined recreational period. I needed to be in tip top shape at all times in order to stay focused and optimistic about the situation.

  The next step is exercising your mental muscles. This is very important to do. I urge everyone who's dealing with a criminal matter to read law books. Educate yourself on the law. Don't depend solely on your attorney. Search the internet for cases that are similar to yours. Buy different books that fit what you are going through. Some of the books that I picked up were *Justice While Black* by Robbin Shipp, Esp. and Nick Chiles and *Arrest Proof Yourself* by Dale C. Carson and Wes Denham.

  The courts usually have exclusive access to the crime scene and they can also easily remove or control the release of exculpatory evidence that may contradict or expose the prosecution's case or raise reasonable doubt. This system is not created to protect you.

  The police are like the gatekeepers to this system. They also get the chance to talk to you and other witnesses first, giving them the power to pressure you into changing your story, through coercion and collusion. This is why it's important to keep your mouth shut.

  The Miranda Warning is not a joke. "You have the right to remain silent. Anything you say can and will be used against you in a court of law. You have the right to an attorney. If you cannot afford an attorney, one will be provided for you. Do you understand the rights I have just read to you? With these rights in mind, do you wish to speak to me?" It is your right to remain silent or say no until an attorney is present.

Prosecutors often trump up charges on defendants as a scare tactic, in hopes that over time, the pressure would break them down and force them to capitulate, or agree, to a plea deal. If the prosecutor can keep the bond high, it will force the defendant to stay in jail until their trial date. In that case, they then have an even better shot at making you capitulate because of the harsh circumstances.

The court has unlimited money, but you don't. Please be mindful of this. The system feeds on the weak and vulnerable, which are usually poor, urban African-Americans. We are easy targets because we are uneducated and born into these broken homes. Most African-American families don't have the financial resources to take their case to trial. So instead, they settle for a plea bargain.

The court also has control of the evidence. Most cases, especially high-profile cases, always gets bound over. The amount of evidence needed to bond stuff over is the bare minimum. What I noticed was that the exculpatory evidence in my favor was withheld intentionally. The videotape was said not to help or hurt me or even work for that matter.

The prosecutor even tried to charge me $3,200 for the medical records. One dollar per page, even though we only wanted the toxicology reports, showing the blood alcohol level! But, of course, since this evidence would hurt her case (showing that the two guys were not in their right state of mind) she made it extremely tough to get those records. Eventually, after months of asking, nagging, and negotiating, we got them for free. It took me seven months to get the medical records from the prosecutor showing that both guys were intoxicated and under the influence of drugs.

After finding out about the video tape, my attorney asked the prosecutor about it. She gave him a copy of a tape that was encrypted and could not play on any laptop. I had to hire a video expert that unencrypted the video and enhanced the images to clarify it. You have to be willing to fight for your life with everything you have and never give up!

When I was finally able to view the video, my mouth dropped. The video showed the driver of the car picking up something on the ground (possibly the gun). Also, it showed him running to the dumpster (possibly disposing the evidence) and throwing something in the trash receptacle next to the pump. None of this matched his story in the preliminary exam.

The grainy video made it hard to make out exactly what the men went to the car and grabbed, but, by his actions, it was clear he wasn't trying to leave the scene. As a matter of fact, he was coming back and even had his hand pointed at me. That is when I fired my first shot. This is how I remembered it.

This leads me to the last, but not least, most important muscle of them all: the spiritual muscle. Now I know people have different beliefs, but my story just might strengthen your faith in a higher power. It is very important that you strengthen your faith during a time of need.

God hasn't brought you this far to let you down.

Church is a place where you should spend your time, even after you get out of your situation. God is the only One who can get you out of this vicious justice cycle. He is the only One who can lead you to make the right decisions when picking legal counsel and the only One who can give you peace of mind.

The Bible is filled with stories and parables that we can relate to our lives. It is a Book full of inspirational stories and allegories. These are examples of situations that we find ourselves in, time and time again. Times change, but the situations stay the same. When you see yourself in these stories, it strengthens your faith in Him.

I saw myself in the story of Job. The righteous Job was blessed with wealth and sons and daughters. Then, God asks Satan for his opinion of Job's righteousness. Satan answers that Job is only faithful because God had blessed him. He said that if God were to take away everything from Job, he would surely curse God.

I had a lot of things going for me and all of a sudden, it was being taken away from me, one-by-one. I felt like everyone counted me out and looked at my position like a piece of meat hanging from a string over a pack of wolves. People were ready to apply for my job. To make matters worse, my daughter's mother saw an opportunity to regain full custody of our daughter.

My relationship with my girlfriend was on the decline because of the shooting. The media tried to destroy my reputation by insinuating that I shot two guys over "Santa's girlfriend." It was hard for her to keep hearing this undertone of a possible relationship with Jasmine. We started trying to lean on each other a lot more, but Jasmine's appreciation for my chivalry became uncomfortable for us both.

Unfortunately, we were off and on during that time. During the "off" periods, I found myself being exactly who they said I was. In fact, when I was modeling, I was told to make sure I kept my marital status as "Single" because it could hurt my modeling career. I wasn't sure how much more would be said about me and Jasmine in court, but I tried to keep the peace with my girlfriend as much as I could.

One day, I observed that the root word of testimony is "test". You cannot have a true testimony without a test. You see, God communicates with us through praying and the Bible. We gain faith and strength through our testimony. I strongly believe this, and I couldn't have made it without God.

Preparing for trial takes all of that. If you love yourself, you'll work hard to protect you, your family and friends from getting caught up in this system. No kind of trouble, intended or unintended, is worth all of this. Trust me!

When I returned to work, I was the topic of discussion. "He's back! How did he get his job back?" People would gossip all around me. "Did he beat the case?" That was the main question most would ask, but I remained silent like I did when I was arrested. I didn't trust anyone and I wasn't supposed to.

People would use the things I said against me in a

heartbeat. Some people are opportunists and they would have loved to see me lose my job so they could apply for my position. I had to be smart and strategic with everything I said. I had to be very discreet when I would charge my tether during my breaks. My phone seemed to hold more charge than my tether device at times. At the end of the day, I would sit in the corner with my cell phone and ankle glued to an outlet.

Often, I would eat in private areas because in the public lunch room, an update of my case would flash across the television screen. "Shooting Santa trial date set." It would read. The camera would show me talking to my attorney, with my hair neatly trimmed and a humble concerned expression.

I had to go through this at least four times as my trial date was constantly pushed back. My hair line would soon follow if this protracted process didn't soon end. Stress is a heavy burden when you're facing prison time. It can be detrimental to your health. I had to keep that in mind.

I would leave work in a hurry to get to the officer to do my weekly check-ins. When I showed up to the jail with my work uniform, I was an anomaly of the crowd. Almost no one had a job in the crowd of tether participants, which probably means that they had nowhere to go urgently. For me, time was of the essence. I had to go to work, to school, to pick my daughter up from school and get her started on her homework. I had a life, and this tether was crippling me.

As time went on and the trial continued to get

postponed, I began to get used to the curfew. Things started to become a bit normal as the media continued to die down. I actually ended up being picked up in Mayor Dave Bing's, Detroit Piston mentor program. I was referred by a friend. The program hand-picked young, troubled Black males to receive one-on-one mentoring. It didn't seem that the case affected their opinion of me. I was excited about the opportunity.

I was used to being around high-profile people, but this was different. I was considered a possible criminal and just charged nine months ago. *"But, hey, maybe my luck is turning around,"* I thought, *"Just maybe!"*

I went to the Detroit Pistons games and set courtside with the kids. We rooted our team on and I watched in awe as these kids enjoyed an experience they never had before – an opportunity to sit courtside at an NBA basketball game. They even got a chance to meet some of the former NBA players, guys like Derrick Coleman and Jalen Rose, who were always there to support this beautiful program.

The energy level was high and the kids enjoyed the ball rolling by their feet as the players dove to the floor to get the ball. We were part of the action and they were getting all kinds of life-changing experiences.

Throughout the time we set courtside, I had to be cognizant that my tether was sometimes showing. With the bright lights and spotlight on us at all times, this was not a good look for a mentor. Especially for a mentor who was associated with a high-profile figure like the Mayor.

Suddenly, the unthinkable happened. The big Jumbotron camera zoomed in on Dave and the crew. The crowd gave a standing ovation for the work we were doing, and on the screen you could see that ugly tether as plain as day. I just knew the whole arena saw it!

I tucked my leg under the chair so far that I thought my leg would snap at the knee. I was embarrassed with chills up my back and neck. My face turned as red as a strawberry. No one seemed to have even noticed it, but in my mind, everyone noticed it! I was so self-conscious of that stupid thing!

As I drove to work the next day, my phone rang. It was Dave's secretary. "Hello Marcus, this is Taryn."

"Hey Taryn!" I said, in good spirits. "What can I do for you?"

"Well, I was calling about the mentor program. You see, your background check came back and..." she paused for a moment that seemed like hours.

"And what?" I said concerned.

"And you have seven felonies pending. We can no longer have you around the teenagers. You've got to take care of that first," she said.

My voice cracked as I tried to defend myself, "But I haven't been convicted of anything and I'm going to beat this case! I...I know I am. I have all the evidence!"

"I'm sorry, Marcus. It's our policy. Pending or not, you cannot be around those kids with those charges," she said firmly, but apologetically.

"I understand," I responded, softly. "I'm guilty until proven innocent."

CHAPTER 11
And So It Begins...The Trial

"In the heat of battle, the mind tends to lose its balance. It is vital to keep your presence of mind, maintaining your mental powers, whatever the circumstances. Make the mind tougher by exposing it to adversity. Learn to detach yourself from the chaos of the battlefield. "

– Robert Greene, The 33 Strategies of War

Day 1

"Guilty!" No one who is on trial wants to hear those words. Your first responsibility in court is to pick the group of people who can be the most objective and hopefully not say that word. Monday was the first day of the trial and we had to pick the jury. The candidates for the jury came into the courtroom, one by one, as we prepared to question them and either choose or dismiss them from serving for the case. It was a very long process. It took about six hours.

We had all kinds of information about each potential juror. We had their occupation, age, and names. We would ask questions like, "Have you ever been in a crime? Has anyone you know ever been in a crime? Have you ever been involved in a self-defense act? Do you carry a pistol for self-defense reasons? Have you ever been shot? Do you have any military experience? Are there any police officers in your family? Have you had any encounters with the police? Have you ever been charged with a felony?"

As I was looking at the jurors, I was always looking to see if there was somebody I can relate to. Each lawyer could strike up to about 10 candidates out for just about any reason except race, gender or sexual orientation. I was honestly looking for somebody who was not of Arabian descent, but I couldn't do it solely on that. Could you blame me? I wanted a fighting chance!

The prosecutor would strike out the candidates that I liked and my lawyer would strike out the candidates I didn't like. There was one white guy who was an electrical engineer who I could identify with. He seemed clean cut. He was wearing khakis, Cole Haan shoes, and a button up shirt. I wasn't just looking for Black people. I only needed one person to believe me and that would create a hung jury, which was the next best thing to all 12 agreeing I was not guilty.

One of the jurors got out of the jury duty by saying, "I don't want to be a part of the jury because I feel that there's too many innocent Black men in jail already." She, of course, was eventually struck off the list. In my head, I felt that was the dumbest thing she could say to the court. I mean, if you really had a problem with Black innocence being ushered away into state cages, here was your opportunity to make a difference and potentially save a Black man from going to prison based on the evidence you hear. Jury duty is an important responsibility. Every citizen should take it seriously. Lives are at stake here!

After breaks and lunch, we had opening arguments. The prosecutor was different, but I later learned that this lady was one of the top lawyers in the Prosecutor's Office. She was very, very good and I heard she would try anything. She was a short, red-headed white woman, with big, thick glasses who looked about 47-years old. She always wore high heels and dark or moderate colors like black, gray or dark blue. She reminded me of a stern school principal.

The prosecutor was well-spoken and very intimidating. "This young man shot four shots into a car after a man accidentally bumped his girlfriend!" She could get her point across with her very convincing emotional arguments. I almost thought I was guilty, listening to her! Unfortunately, my lawyer's opening argument was not as impressive.

That day, I went home and couldn't eat or sleep. Unfortunately, I picked up a bad habit. I started smoking, too. The drinking and smoking was taking its toll on my physically. I even lost weight, and I couldn't afford to lose any weight. I went from 162 lbs. to 149 lbs. Remember, I had to stuff a Santa Claus suit to even be laughable as a fat guy. That night, as I was sitting on the porch, I began shaking uncontrollably. I was sitting, and then I would get up and pace back and forth. I would cry and then stop. Pace and then stop. It was torture.

Monday: The People – 1 Point, Marcus – 0 Points

Day 2

Beep! Beep! Beep! I walked in through the metal detectors, which beeped immediately as it recognized my tether. My family was behind me to support me. At the beginning of the day, the prosecutor offered me a plea bargain for one year in jail. She must have told my lawyer something like, "He can take this plea for one year in jail because I'm about to get in that ass. He can get out on good behavior. He'll have seven felonies on his record, but then he can go back to regular society." Mr. Craig pulled me aside to explain the offer.

My mother was all in. She was like a secretary the way she helped organize my paperwork and evidence for my attorney. Both of my parents were at every meeting and every court date making sure the court wouldn't railroad their son. My mom was on top of everything the lawyer said. So, it was no surprise that she noticed my attorney pull me to the corner to ask me a scary question.

"They are offering you a plea deal for one year in the County Jail, Marcus. You could get out in 6 months on good behavior." My heart stopped as I replied. "But I thought we were going to trial? We got this case in the bag right?" My attorney said, "No case is for sure. I mean, I don't know what those jurors are thinking. I think it's a good deal, considering the fact that you are facing a minimum of fifteen years in prison if you lose this trial. The prosecutor is calling this the Virgil Smith deal."

Virgil Smith, Jr. was a member of the Michigan Senate, who was recently sentenced to one year in jail as a plea bargain for shooting up his girlfriend's car. "But, I'm not Virgil Smith!" I yelled. "I'm not taking it. We are going to trial!"

My mom came over and questioned me, "What is going on?"

"They offered me a plea deal and I said 'no'. I don't really want to talk about it," I said, brushing her off. I was upset. I felt that my attorney was leaning towards me taking that deal. Was he no longer confident in this case?

My attorney came to me three times with that deal and I kept denying it. My whole life would be messed up. I would lose my daughter, my job and my freedom! Considering the fact that I was facing 15 years, my attorney thought I should at least think about it. I looked him dead in the eye and said, "I'm going in this Lion's Den and, like Daniel, I'm getting out!" One year versus fifteen years doesn't sound bad, but it's still prison and I wasn't interested.

In the courtroom, prosecution came in and began making her case. She first passed out some pictures of the men's gunshot wounds. The pictures eventually made it around to me. If I had any appetite left, it definitely would have been gone at that point. The black vehicle was full of broken glass and bullet holes. The quagmire of blood that surrounded the car was a terrible sight.

The pictures of one man's forearm nearly ripped off the bone and his fingers hanging on by a thread of carnage was tough to look at. But looking at the other man with a tube down his throat with his stomach opened up on the operating table was a sight that will be burned into my memory for life. He looked like a busted open watermelon dripping with a white, frothy spoiled yogurt. There was also a bullet wound to his leg which tore through the muscle and flesh like a meat grinder at a slaughterhouse.

The next picture was the weapon in question – my firearm. The tool that was used to create this carnage. With that picture, she made it seem as if I was the only one with a gun. She tried to draw attention away from the fact that these guys, too, were armed and started the entire altercation.

The prosecutor then called her first witness, Mr. Ramad. He was the second guy in the car who was shot in the hand. He didn't have a sling on this time, but he said he had a metal plate in his arm. She began asking him questions and stating what she thought happened that night.

"And then, he ran to the dumpster to take cover!" She put that out there because in the video, his friend ran to the dumpster, but he didn't talk about that during the pre-trial.

"What were you doing out so late at night?" the prosecutor asked. "We were killing the night and stopped to get some water at the gas station."

"Did you drink anything that night?"

"Earlier in the day, I drank two beers."

"At the gas station, what happened?"

"My buddy got out and asked me, 'Hey, do you want anything.' I said, 'No, I don't want anything.' And then he backed up and accidentally bumped this girl that was at the window. Then, a guy got in his face and pulled a gun out. My buddy started to run to the car and he just started opening fire."

"Do you see the guy who shot you in the courtroom?" The prosecutor asked.

"Yes, he's right there in the black suit!" he yelled as he pointed right at me. The prosecutor turned and pointed at me and said, "Mr. Weldon shot you!" She always pointed her finger at me and looked me dead in the eye. Every time that prosecutor pointed her finger at me, the entire courtroom's eyes would follow. All the attention would be focused on me, like I was some caged animal in the zoo.

They kept describing me. Black suit. Black tie. White shirt. Everybody was looking at me like, "Oooo, looks like you're going down, buddy." The aggressiveness from the prosecutor's voice was intimidating, so intimidating that my family and friends could feel it. My friend, Beanie, told me later that she was so terrifying that he felt he was the one in the chair facing life.

During cross-examination, my attorney asked Ramad some tough questions,

"We're going to walk you back down into that night. Now, you're saying you had two beers. At first, you said you hadn't had any alcohol at all. Is that correct? Are you saying that because you knew that alcohol would show up on your toxicology report? Is that why you admitted you had two beers now?"

"Well, I didn't want to lie," he responded in an uncomfortable tone. Mr. Ramad's demeanor was dreadful.

He had jeans on and didn't even iron his shirt. He had no court etiquette at all. Court etiquette is critical for demonstrating your character.

"There was a lot of media attention on this. I didn't want to say that I was drinking because I was embarrassed. I'm Muslim. I'm not supposed to drink. I didn't want to embarrass myself in front of my community," he said, somewhat humbly.

"Oh, so you perjured yourself? Right? Let me show you your toxicology report. It says here that you were a tad bit over the legal limit of alcohol, which means you shouldn't even have been driving that night. If you had been pulled over, you would have gotten a DUI ticket. Technically, you shouldn't have even made it to the gas station checking any prices or getting water. You should have been in jail!"

My attorney was on a roll. *"Marcus is gaining a point right about now,"* I thought to myself. "Anything else you do tonight? Narcotics, perhaps? No? Ok, Mr. Ramad. What's this? Marijuana!"

"I didn't smoke no weed!" Ramad retorted.

"Then, why is it in your system?" Mr. Craig questioned him sternly. While Ramad was on the stand, he kept rotating in his chair which, according to the judge, was something to look out for. The sign of someone possibly lying was fidgeting and rotating in the chair.

"Your Honor, I object!" The prosecutor didn't want my lawyer to continue. "How long can marijuana stay in your system?" she asked.

"Overruled. Counselor continue," the judge allowed my lawyer to finish.

"But, it is in your system, right?" my lawyer interrogated further.

"I might have smoked some weed a couple of days ago. I didn't want to embarrass the Muslim community," Ramad responded, clearly knowing he wasn't looking so good for lying either before today or lying today.

My attorney then questioned him about the actual shooting. He couldn't remember his original testimony and kept saying that he was in pain so he may have said some things, but now he couldn't confirm them. My attorney continued asking him about his original statement that his friend went to get a baseball bat. There was no baseball bat. My attorney kept harping on it so much so that the judge said, "That's enough, Mr. Craig!"

My lawyer asked him where his friend was (the one who was messing with Jasmine). "He is back in Yemen with his family," Ramad responded. This dude left the country! I couldn't believe it. Now, he couldn't come back to Detroit because all flights between Yemen and Detroit were cancelled. *"Isn't that convenient?"* I thought.

My lawyer continued. "How did your friend bump into the young lady?"

"Well, he booty-bumped her," Ramad replied.

"Oh so you were driving, killing the night and he booty-bumped her? What does that mean?" Mr. Craig asked the same question I was asking in my head.

"Well, his butt kinda hit her butt." Ramad's choice of words was horrible!

The jury asked questions as well. They had good questions, too. They wanted to know if his buddy was a drinker also. This man actually said he didn't know. They were friends for nine years. Who doesn't know whether or not their friends drink?

The next witness was the officer who was the partner of the officer who testified during the preliminary. He explained that they pulled up to get gas and saw a Dodge Charger. This was the Arabian guy's car. Then, he claimed they heard shots and they looked up and a guy in a Santa suit was letting shots go.

"Did you see anybody else shooting?"

"No, I didn't."

"Did you see any shots take affect?"

"No, I didn't."

"Did you hear any arguing?"

"No, I didn't."

His comments weren't the same as he originally stated in his police report. The jury had questions then.

"Did Mr. Weldon shoot before Mr. Abdallah got to the car or after?"

"After."

"Did you see Mr. Abdallah reach for anything?"

"No, I didn't see him reach for anything." There were not many questions after that.

The way the officers spoke, sounded like they were watching a movie. They were coming from a Christmas party so they weren't on duty. They also admitted to drinking, but only one or two beers. So, everybody only drank one or two beers, huh?

I had my lawyer on one side of me and my private detective on the other side. We hadn't called any witnesses on my behalf yet. The prosecutor's witnesses didn't help her case as much as she would have liked. One perjured himself. The other didn't seem as reliable. The video was also shown to the jury. The whole courtroom could see what they saw. I just hope they had the same video I had. We collectively agreed that today was a good day, but to me, it felt like a tie.

I went back home still stressed. I didn't have as many cigarettes. I remember thinking, *"I think I can deal with just one. I'm not trying to get addicted to these things."* I ate a little bit. I had some celery, a plum and some noodles. I tried to eat something heavy, but I just couldn't keep it down. I would spit it all back up. I just had too much anxiety. I took medication just to go to sleep. Benadryl was my number one friend.

My mother, father, church members, my girlfriend and a few others, about 15, came with me to court every day. I was getting texts from people daily. My family and immediate friends who went to court with me were the only ones I texted back.

Tuesday: The People – 2 Points, Marcus – 1 Point

Day 3

The first witness was the cop who testified in the preliminary trial. He gave the exact same testimony he gave during the pre-trial. He said he saw it all happen. My lawyer said, "You realize we have video on this, right?" Mr. Craig was very calm during his interrogation. I kept wondering why he wouldn't dig into the witnesses because he could have really gone after these guys. The prosecutor objected at least 15 times every five minutes! It didn't seem like a fair fight.

"So, you heard four to seven shots? Where did the other shots come from? It sounds like to me there could have been another gun here. Did you search the area?" Mr. Craig asked calmly.

"No, we didn't," the officer replied.

What kind of officer shows up at a place where shooting was going on and not search the area for evidence?

The jury had to be as confused as I was. The only thing that mattered was finding evidence that the Arabian guys had guns and were shooting at me like I was shooting at them. Finally, I told my lawyer to ask a very pointed question that he didn't want to ask because he thought the officer would lie. I didn't care. I wanted the answer to the question on record.

"Did you search the dumpster? Did you secure the scene?"

"No," the officer said.

I figured he hadn't because he didn't have a picture of the dumpster like he did of everything else. Another witness for the prosecution was the Arabian guys' doctor. When the doctor got on the stand and began to testify, he started crying.

"I thought the guy wasn't gonna walk again. I

thought he was gonna die," the doctor said. Clearly, he was coached. My attorney began the cross-examination.

"I want you to read this toxicology report. Read that for me. What does that mean?"

"It means, Mr. Abdallah was two to three times over the legal limit of alcohol consumption for drivers."

Two beers can't make you that drunk. If I could have texted someone in that moment, my text would have been "LOL".

Next, the forensic officer testified. He got on the stand and said that the bullets he found from the gun were destroyed very badly. He found 4 bullets and said that 2 of them for sure came from my gun and there were two others.

"But it's most likely they came from Mr. Weldon's gun, right?" the prosecutor said, leading the witness. "I can't say for sure. I just can't."

When my attorney cross-examined him, he asked, "What you're saying is that there's a possibility of another gun out there?"

"It possibly could have been," the officer replied.

"So, you can't say for sure that all of these bullets came from my client's gun?"

"No, I can't," he answered.

The prosecutor was mad. I won that day!

Wednesday: The People – 2 Points, Marcus – 2 Points

Day 4

It was time for my defense. The day before we were going to submit the 911 recording of the clerk stating guns were being fired, the judge kicked the recording out. He said the 911 tape would not be admissible because the clerk was not in the courtroom. Are you serious?! The clerk couldn't be found in the past year and a half. He quit his job and moved. My attorney asked to have some of the charges removed. Each charge had at least a minimum of a 5-year sentence. So, I started the 4th day of the trial with the same seven felony charges I had at the beginning. None of them had been dropped.

We put Jasmine on the stand first that day. Jasmine is the star of the show. This was her first day in court because witnesses cannot sit in the courtroom during the trial. When she walked in the room, I immediately felt an uncanny awkwardness. There was a situation that went down that only a few of us knew about.

My attorney was able to examine her first. She made a phenomenal statement describing the situation. She explained how she thought the man accidentally bumped her, but then it turned into pushing and she said, "Excuse me," several times. He didn't acknowledge her.

Then, I came over and said, "Hey!" Then, he pushed me and I almost fell back, and I pushed him off of me because he was in my face. Jasmine yelled, "Excuse me!" Then, the man turned around and Jasmine heard him say, "I got something for you!" as he went to his car. He started digging under the seat. Jasmine froze. I shouted,

"Jasmine! Run!"

"The next thing I knew, I heard shots and bullets were whizzing past me as I ran away from the gas station. I thought I was going to be shot in the back. I kept checking behind me to see if I had gotten shot. I kept imagining myself getting shot and dying," Jasmine recounted her experiences of that dreadful night.

"Did you see a gun?" my attorney asked.

"No, I didn't see a gun, but when he went to the car, I knew what time it was. I froze. Marcus snapped me out of it and, if it wasn't for Marcus, I probably would have been shot."

The judge asked the jury if they had any questions. They didn't. After that, the judge ordered a break for lunch. The prosecutor was furious. She wanted to cross-examine before recess. "Your honor! Since we're going into recess, I don't want the witness anywhere near the family of Mr. Weldon. They are already talking in the hallway about this case. If the jury hears them, it will compromise the case. Ms. Paige is a very important witness to this case and I think she should be in the witness room and not be able to leave out."

The judge replied, "I can't keep anyone back from having lunch."

"Well, she should not have any contact with them!"

"Ms. Paige?" the judge called Jasmine, "Please stay away from Mr. Weldon and his family."

After lunch, the prosecutor cross-examined Jasmine. The first thing she asked her was, "Did you have sexual relations with Mr. Weldon?" Now, what does that have to do with anything?! I could feel eyes from everybody, including my girlfriend, burning the back of my neck. Needless to say, I did not turn around to confirm it.

Jasmine paused for what seemed like ten seconds. Ten seconds is a long time in court. If she didn't say yes, they would all think she was lying. Finally, she answered, "Yes."

"Was this before or after the incident?"

"After," Jasmine softly replied.

This was embarrassing. I was praying, "Lord, if I get through this, I will never, in my life, go out again. I will just stay in the house! I'm done with the night life. I don't even care. I'm not going back to that job and this girl right here, I'm not dealing with anymore!"

It wasn't fair, but in that moment, I was blaming Jasmine for the whole thing.

The truth is, after the shooting, things really heated up with me and Jasmine. We became closer because of the situation and we were both in a very vulnerable state. Everything before this was normal. We were friends only. Neither of us looked at each other in any other type of way other than friends. Or did we?

It wasn't long before Jasmine and I became intimate with each other, which became a problem, of course, in my relationship. I was selfish and between the alcohol and depression, compromised our trust and used the excuses of our fights and temporary break ups to justify my sexual behavior.

I just knew the prosecutor would play dirty and

question our relationship. She was looking for anything to destroy our character and embarrass the both of us in front of my family and friends.

The prosecutor continued with Jasmine asking her about her statement she made the night of the shooting. The prosecutor tried to elude that because of our sexual relationship Jasmine was making things up and she wasn't scared that night.

"You weren't even scared that night! You never once said in your statement that you were scared. You said you were agitated. You said you were confused. You never once said you were scared when the pushing started. You never said you thought you were going to be kidnapped. But now that you have a sexual relationship with Marcus, you want to come to his defense!"

My attorney objected and noted that it was three or four o'clock in the morning and clearly Jasmine was crying and under a lot of stress right after the shooting. The judge honored the objection.

"I don't know if Mr. Weldon is going to take the stand or not, but this is my prime witness," the prosecutor said. She didn't know if I was going to take the stand or not because most people do not take the stand in their own defense. George Zimmerman didn't go on the stand. Your lawyer is supposed to be your voice.

The whole time, I was writing. I was either taking notes or drawing, but I wanted to look busy and engaged in the case. I wanted to be perceived as being serious about this case. If you're ever in this situation, make sure you are very engaged in your own case. Nobody is going to defend you better than you.

The jury didn't have any questions for Jasmine. Not one. All of their questions for the day were for the prosecution's witnesses. I thought Jasmine held her ground and told the truth. That's all I needed to help me.

My attorney and I brainstormed what we had left in our arsenal. I had my friend, Josh, who worked at Border Patrol. The prosecutor tried to block him from getting on stand with his badge and firearm showing. She asked him, "Are you on duty? If not take off your badge and gun." Keep in mind that other police officers who took the stand wore their uniform. Customs border patrol officers are in federal jobs and always on duty.

Anyway, the reason she did not want him to speak on my character with the badge is because that would have made the jury lean more to my side. It would have shown I have a good character. Good people hang together. I also had Rick Ector, Self-Defense expert, but the judge wouldn't let me use him either. The prosecutor said his thoughts were just his opinion. Our strategy was to use him as a character witness instead. That way, we still get his thoughts, but with a different twist.

I would go home every day and think about the strategy for the next day. Friday was supposed to be my last day in court. There was a possibility that the trial could go over and we'd have to start again the following week. I didn't want that. All of a sudden, I had an epiphany. I thought about interviewing the officer who came to the scene after the shooting to take statements from all eye-witnesses. "We can ask him the questions he asked the clerk," I said. "That's a great idea, Marcus!" my attorney said.

"Put me in coach!" I told Mr. Craig to let me go on the stand. I was ready.

I ran through the story about working and leaving the property. I told them about the flat tire. Finally, I got to the scene everyone was talking about. I explained that in the process of pushing back and forth, my firearm was sliding down my pants. "I gave the man a warning and said I was armed. Then, he went to the car, reached under the seat and pulled out a gun."

"Did you see what kind of gun was it?"

"It was a black gun. It was dark and I really couldn't tell what kind it was. It was kinda small. It looked like a revolver. He pointed the gun at me and fired a shot. I fired back. He fired again. I was backing up as I was firing. I wasn't really sure I hit him at all."

I just established that there was another gun. No one else had said there was another gun. The prosecutor tried to get one of the officers to say that all of the bullets found came from my gun. We couldn't use the 911 tape where the clerk talked about another gun because, once again, the clerk wasn't at the trial. Rick Ector couldn't be a witness because his review of the case was considered an opinion based on evidence that was not officially a part of the case. All of that would have been hearsay. But, now that I've established there was another gun, we can talk about another gun. For a moment, I felt good about the next day.

As we left out of court, we saw an ambulance leaving the County Jail. I didn't think anything of it because the day had worn on me, but I was feeling positive. When I got home, I received a phone call from my friend Rome's son. Rome was one of those friends who was in a bad situation like me. Rome's son said, "Pops committed suicide." I was like, "Why?" "He was in the County. They tried to get him a plea deal, but he didn't believe the jury would believe him. He already had previous felonies against him," he said, sorrowfully.

I could not believe that he did that. On the other hand, it crossed my mind several times, but I threw the thoughts out of the window. Not Rome. His son told me when the funeral would be and where the candlelight vigil was going to be. I sat in astonishment. My anxiety was already out of control. I couldn't endure a funeral during all of this.

Thursday: The People – 2 Points, Marcus – 3 Points

Day 5

On Friday, the prosecutor was ready to cross-examine me. "We're gonna cut straight to the chase. Why didn't you tell 911 there was a shootout?" she asked me.

"I didn't get a chance to because there was a car following me. I started running. I thought it was the Arabian guys chasing me."

"You didn't hear them say, 'Stop! Police!'?"

"No. I didn't see any lights. I didn't see any badges. All I saw was a black car following me. Why would I stop?" I answered.

She tried to get me to admit that I ran from them while they were saying, "Police! Police!" Even if that were the case, the way things are going now, stopping for the police isn't something that's going to save your life any more than running from them. At the time, I was thinking, whoever is chasing me will be shot before I get shot.

Then, the prosecutor tried to get me to admit when I had the gun in my hand using the video. I couldn't see anything because the video was so small. "I don't know what that is. I'm sorry," I stated matter-of-factly.

"Well," the prosecutor continued, "show me here on the video where they shot."

Finally, she enlarged the video. One of the jurors got off of his seat and came and stood right next to me. I started pointing and seeing where he shot and you could see his hand pointed right at me. But you couldn't see any guns in the video because the equipment was so old and the camera quality was poor. The video made us look like little Mario Brothers from the Nintendo game. That didn't even matter. I made my case. Yes, I had a gun and I shot it, but somebody was shooting at me. The jury had no questions for me.

Now that we established that there was another gun, my attorney could call the investigating officer who came on the scene. "Did you say to the clerk, *'This is an investigation. Do you understand that?'*" my attorney began.

"Yes, I did," the officer responded.

"Did you say to the clerk, *'Did you see what happened?'* that night?"

"Yes."

"Did you say to the clerk, *'Do you know the guy in the Santa suit?'*?"

"Yes, I did."

"Did you ask him, *'Did you see the Santa guy's gun?'*?"

"Yes, I did."

"Did you say to the clerk, *'Did you see who was firing the second gun?'*?"

BINGO! We couldn't get him to answer the question because the clerk wasn't there to give his testimony. But, we could get the question out there that demonstrates there was a second gun. Then, the jury asked some questions, "Why did you ask, *'Did you see who fired the second gun?'*? Can you read all of the answers to the questions, please? Did you just guess that there was a second gun? Did you believe there was a second gun?"

The officer had to read his answers to the questions.

"I asked the clerk if he saw who fired the second gun because he said he heard secondary gun fire."

"Objection, your Honor! He heard secondary gun fire. He didn't see a second gun!" The judge let the officer continue.

"Read the answers to the questions," the judge ordered.

The officer continued, "The clerk said, *'I heard two shots from the direction of the Arabian male toward the Santa guy, and I heard four to five shots from the direction of the Santa guy toward the Arabian males.'"*

My attorney asked, "What did the [off-duty] officers who were there that night say they heard?"

"About five to eight shots," the investigating officer replied. That's about right, I thought. I wanted to kick my feet up, put them on the table and lean back in satisfaction, but it wasn't over yet.

The prosecutor was furious right now. She called her last witnesses. There was a video expert who analyzed the video and said the video we had was fabricated. She didn't want to use our video, which I spent a lot of money on, but it was much clearer. In my video, you could see what the Arabian guy had in his hand and that he ran to the dumpster. "Yes, the video they had was fabricated. The video skips," the video expert says.

Then, the prosecutor called the off-duty officers to the stand. "Did you hear any secondary gun fire?" she asks. "No, I didn't hear any secondary gun fire," they answered riskily.

"Are you trained in hearing secondary gun fire?"

"Yes, I'm trained."

"So, you didn't hear any secondary gunfire?"

For the first time during the trial, my attorney got extremely loud. "Objection, Your Honor! So you're telling me that these are the same officers that say they didn't see the Arabian guys get in the car. They didn't see the guy reach into the car. And we have video showing all of this happening. Now you're expecting me to believe that these guys right here are telling the truth? It's probably safe to say that you didn't see everything. Let me ask you a question officer. How much coaching has the prosecution done with you? Did she call you last night and say what she wanted you to say? As a matter of fact, when you were in the back hallway, did she say to you, 'I really need you to say this so we can get this young man locked up.'? Is that true?"

Of course, the officers denied being coached. My attorney lit into them. The jury really paid attention because my attorney was really making a scene and he hadn't for the entire week. The officers tried to be really calm, but they were clearly embarrassed.

"This is a disgrace. You're sitting here. You're lying. You're police officers, but no one searched the scene. This is terrible!" The prosecutor was yelling, "Objection! Objection!" I'm thinking, *"Get 'em, Mr. Craig! Get 'em!"*

The jury asked a very important question. "Is it possible because the video skips that it missed the flare or flash on the tape?" The prosecutor kept saying there was no flash on the tape coming from the Arabian guy's direction. "Isn't that right, officers, that if there was a gunshot you'd see a flash on the tape?"

"Yeah, you'll see a flash," the officers responded.

"Objection, Your Honor! These are officers, not video experts!" Mr. Craig rightly points out. The judge advised us that the video expert had gone home for the day.

"Well," Mr. Craig said, "I have a video expert in the hallway. Let's ask him." Power move! I had a video expert in place and ready just in case.

The video expert took the stand and the jury asked him the question,

"Is it possible that because the video skips that it missed the flare or flash on the tape?" The video expert said, "Yes, because the flash is a millisecond and the tape jumps around. You can throw an apple in the air and the next scene it will be half way on the ground and the next scene it will be on the ground. It won't show the apple's full motion. It's like a slide show."

The prosecutor was furious and started snapping her fingers.

"So, you're saying the video would be going like this and it's not going to catch that gun fire?"

"Yeah," he said, "Just like you're snapping your fingers and have that space in between those snaps. That's the gunfire. The video can jump and miss things just like that."

"No further questions, your Honor," she said. I guess the prosecution rests?

After that, the attorneys delivered their closing arguments. Each had 45 minutes. The prosecutor went first for 20 minutes. The Defense goes next for 45 minutes. Then the prosecution goes again, so she planned finished the final 25 minutes after Mr. Craig. That sucks. But, Mr. Craig had a powerful closing argument. It needed to be filmed.

"You heard a witness sit in this chair and lie about drinking because he didn't want to embarrass himself in front of his family. You heard police officers sit in this chair and just contradict everything that's on the video. You heard Ms. Paige answer very personal questions about her life and she told the truth. You know why? She doesn't want to lie on the stand. Not because she wants to embarrass herself. She said to herself, 'I'm not going to perjure myself. I'm not going to lie.' You heard character witnesses on behalf of Mr. Weldon. The doctor has seen countless gunshot wounds, but this one he was crying about. Finally, you heard from a video expert," my attorney ended his argument quite well.

In her closing argument, the prosecutor asked why I didn't shoot a warning shot. That's illegal. You cannot discharge your firearm unless your life is in danger. If I had said I shot a warning shot, I would have been in jail already.

At the end of the day, two jurors were removed. We selected 14 in case something happened to any of them. There were 6 African Americans, of which 2 were women, 1 Latino female, seven were White males. The two that were dismissed were African American men. How convenient is that? I felt good about today, but it still wasn't over.

Friday: The People – 2 Points, Marcus – 4 Points

CHAPTER 12
Father's Day Weekend

"Privileged kids go to counseling. Poor kids go to jail."

– Judge Greg Mathis

After taking a mental beating all week, I had to endure the hardest part of it all. I had to wait for the verdict over the Father's Day weekend and pray that the jury gets it right.

I felt confident in our performance. Our defense was solid but it's always the fear of the unknown that makes you nervous, right?

One thing the Judge said to the jury was that good character was enough to exonerate you. Well, what is "good character"? Character is defined as "the aggregate of features and traits that form the individual nature of some person or thing." So, how can a jury determine if you have good character? This is where it gets tricky.

In my opinion, this is where the unconscious biases affect the decision making of jury members, especially when it comes to Black males. If your mind is primed with bad stereotypes of Black men having violent character, then you may lean towards believing that the Black male is guilty of the crime.

If you don't have family (mother and father) in the

courthouse supporting you, then you send a message to the jury that no one cares about you. So why should they? It is important to have a family and a community around you that can prepare you properly for the world around you. If you come to court dressed in street clothes attire you send a message that you don't care about what happens to you. Finally, if you have a previous record, then the courts will surely bring it up to prove you are a criminal. They will even take pictures off your Facebook page to taint your image. Images and voiced opinions influence our brains. Your reputation is everything. Guard it with your life!

    Throughout the weekend, I would get calls from family members asking if was I okay and how I felt about my chances of winning now that the back and forth was over. I told them I felt good but, every so often, that fear of the unknown would creep back up and bite me. If I told you that I didn't think about suicide once that weekend, I would be lying. However, I understand that suicide can be a thought and it was up to me not to make it a reality.

    I remember sitting around the house in the dark and looking at my phone hoping that Dr. West or Dr. Dyson would call me. I sent Dr. Umar Johnson and C.J. Grisham a text saying, "The verdict is Monday. Pray for me." My hope was to make as many people aware as I could of what may happen. C.J. responded by saying, "I have faith everything will work out." In less, than ten hours my life was going to change for better or for worse.

    I spoke frequently with C.J. throughout that weekend. He was sharing my story on his Facebook page repeatedly. He kept me encouraged by sharing personal stories of things he went through during his trial. I was impressed with C.J.'s level of support and I can honestly say he had a big impact on me. I mean he was a white man who didn't even know me, but still showed true altruism in helping me. "Putting yourself in other people's shoes is the way we can change our country," I told him.

You see, C.J. experienced police misconduct just like a lot of Black people have. Therefore, he had an open mind to both sides. Our cases had some similarities for sure. We both had police officers lie on the stand about us. I could see that I met an unlikely friend through this unfortunate calamity.

As Father's Day Sunday approached, I began to think about the past thirteen months. I thought about when I took my daughter out to a Michigan water park one hot, summer day. It was 100° Fahrenheit outside and we both were dying to get in a pool. I remember watching her swim while I sat poolside with one leg in and one leg out praying that waves didn't go over her head. I couldn't submerge my tether in water, but you better believe if it came to my baby or the tether, I would just have to spend the $1,500 for destroying the device!

People would walk past me, looking at the box on my ankle, while I splashed water from the sidelines looking like a convicted felon. My girlfriend would swim out in the pool with my daughter and keep her company. She supported me as much as she could. I knew this case was killing her inside. I wished we could go back to normal, but this house arrest routine and not being able to fully enjoy myself in various family activities became normal.

My daughter witnessed her father go through a lot. From the media blitz and the stressful breakdowns, to the police sometimes surrounding the house to do random checks to see if I had somehow taken the tether off my leg. One day, while she was on her bike, two unmarked police cars pulled up. The officers jumped out and demanded me to show my ankle and empty my pockets. Two officers stayed by the driveway and two remained by the porch just in case I decided to run.

The traumatizing experiences would always lead my daughter into a plethora of questions. "Why do police officers come over to talk to you daddy?" she would ask. All these things were happening while she watched and listened to the news about police shootings. You can imagine how a 6-year-old would react in a state of confusion. I sat in reflection, wondering if this would be my last Father's Day that weekend. It was up to twelve people to make the right decision and exonerate me on all seven charges so I could be around for every Father's Day for the rest of my daughter's childhood.

I always considered myself a leader because I never wanted to follow the inclinations of others. Instead, I wanted to be a trendsetter. I realized that if I wanted to be a strong leader, I needed to be able to overcome adversity. Adversity is what builds strong leaders and, without it, you are never really tested or challenged. How you handle troubling and trying times determines whether you are even fit to be a leader. I had to remember what I learned in church about how God never gives you more than you can handle. So many times, we lose sight of that when we face adversity and we give up because we believe we are in this alone.

If I considered myself a true leader, I thought that I should welcome these problems with an optimistic mind set. I started thinking of this as a chance to flex my muscles and show that I was built for this. Almost everything precious and of value to me on this earth had been through the fire. I thought about diamonds and the process carbon goes through becoming a diamond. You need the fire and pressure to be a precious diamond. I had no shortage of either!

While reading books, I realized I was unique because I was able to see the bad, the good and the hope in hopelessness. I welcomed the challenge, because I was preparing all my life for this opportunity to prove myself. *"Let's see how strong I really am,"* I thought. I didn't think I was built for this mentally and spiritually. I tried to watch people's mistakes and learn from them. My experiences were my best teachers in life. I bumped my head plenty of times, but my scars showed me I could get through whatever the Devil threw at me.

I also reflected on what I had done wrong in life. I was no angel and I brought a lot of backlash on myself because of bad decisions. On this Father's Day weekend, I finally forgave my daughter's mother and even sent a text apologizing for my wrong doings. I was determined that, after I got out of this fire, I would be a new man.

I began to replay the last 18 months in my head. The video was the evidence that demonstrated the driver had picked up objects off the ground, ran to the dumpster and then tossed something else into a trashcan. Detroit police officers didn't search the scene, nor did they study the video, or else, they would have understood the situation a little more clearly and potentially could have found the gun.

"*Now, with all these police shootings going on and police officers claiming self-defense,*" I thought, "*Why would this be any different? How am I a clean cut, hard-working citizen, not getting the benefit of the doubt here?*" I began to role-play in my head. I took myself out of the video and put a police officer in my position. What would he have done and would it be justified?

A man gets into a physical altercation with an officer, then he runs to his car and grabs an object under the seat and turns toward the officer. Even if it wasn't a gun, the man wouldn't have even made it to the car let, alone come back. The officer would be cleared and placed on a leave of absence. Police officers are advised by their union lawyers not to make a statement after a shooting. They are also usually given 48 to 72 hours before they have to make their official statement. I advise everyday citizens to do the same. Don't jump out there and make an incriminating statement without legal counsel.

When a citizen uses his or her weapon, their actions are heavily questioned. Did he follow the rules completely? Did he overkill? Was he intoxicated? I understand the questions, and I agree that they should be asked, but what makes police officers' stories more believable? Does a badge give you the right to shoot first and ask questions later?

We all are human and have the ability to lie, but given that the justice system backs the police officer's "word" it's easier for them to get away with murder – literally. I respect police officers and think they should get paid more than they do, but there are some bad apples in the bunch.

Among other things, I was also thinking, if I were convicted, what would be my daughter's financial position? I would save as much cash as possible and then convert it into assets and precious metals in hopes to protect it from inflation. This would be strictly for my daughter if the unthinkable were to happen. At least she would have a little money along with the college fund I started saving the day she was born. I was always a proactive thinker when it came to my baby girl.

I thought about all the times the tether went off while I was out. If I were out just a few minutes past my curfew, the loud shouting of a militant voice embarrassed me, demanding my whereabouts. The speaker on the tether reminded me of the old Nextel phones we used to carry in high school. The tether would first vibrate like a cell phone, then the speaker would start this annoying noise followed up by an alarm clock-like noise. The outdated equipment would even go off for no reason sometimes. Just imagine being in a quiet movie theater or a meeting with your boss and this archaic device interrupts you. "What is your location, Mr. Weldon?" they would ask.

One day there was an Amber Alert initiated for a

lost child in the Detroit area. All the tethers in that area went off including mine. I laid in the bed, suddenly scared half to death by the high pitch voice that demanded to know my status. I was always on edge around people hoping that my box would not abruptly introduce itself to everyone in the room.

In my reflections, and while talking to C.J., I thought about my rights as a gun owner. C.J. and I talked about how more African Americans need to know the Second Amendment if they choose to carry a firearm. "There's different protection out there that will help pay for your legal fees," he said to me. The reason why many Black people are not aware about this is that we do not go to follow-up training on firearms or get information from different gun groups.

Many of the people who donated money for my defense were from these gun groups. I experienced a bit of culture shock from these unexpected allies. They re-educated me on the firearms and the gun laws. I learned that I was depriving myself of valuable information by not interacting with them. Firearm Legal Protection was available to me, but I'd never even heard of it because I was not involved in the gun community. If you choose to bear arms, you need to be proactive in expanding your knowledge on the subject of firearms including safety, how to legally carry, and the legal ramifications of using your firearm.

Culture shocks are important to have in your life. One of my heroes, Malcolm X, experienced a culture shock in Mecca that changed his life. He came back to

America with a different outlook on other races. If a guy like Malcolm can turn the corner and deal with cognitive dissonance, we can all learn from him and do the same.

As Americans, we need to be more comfortable around all different cultures if we intend on living in this multiracial melting pot together. The fact that someone is a different hue or comes from a different area shouldn't be a factor of division. Sometimes when I think about this, I want to yell at the top of my lungs, "Let's mitigate the unconscious biases! Black America, let's do our part and take responsibility for our own actions as well. No more looking at ourselves as victims! Instead we should look at ourselves as survivors who've played a major role in building this great nation. Let's take responsibility and start mentoring at least one kid in our neighborhood. Together, if we can put aside our cultural differences to become just one America, this would be a better nation!"

C.J. asked me how more African Americans can get involved with Second Amendment Rights supporters. My response was, "If you want the Black community to be more involved, you've got to make an effort to understand our situation and our plight." My theory is that if anyone really wants to reach out to the Black community, they need to get involved in our communities.

From what I can see, supplying water to Flint, Michigan, or creating job opportunities in the city of Detroit, is done only to fit personal agendas. Someone should consider opening up shooting ranges in the communities, gun safety courses, or implement firearm safety in schools. I mean, think about it, some Detroit kids come across illegal firearms all of the time. How about educating them on these firearms and what to do when you come across one in your household or neighborhood? Many kids are injuring themselves or even mistakenly killing their brother or sister because they don't have a clue about gun safety. Guns are interesting to them because of what they see on tv.

As I spoke with C.J., and other guys in the gun community, I saw this as a chance to unite us as a people. If we had open minds, we could eradicate some of the racism and unconscious biases we have against each other. I know some believe gun groups are racist. I admit I haven't met or talked to every gun organization, but from our conversations, C.J. and his videos seemed to be genuine.

I think that in order for people of all races in the gun community, or any community, to come together we need to have honest dialogue with each other. No one should get upset and start name-calling. We should remember that we all come from different demographics, religions and backgrounds so we will have different outlooks on life. I'm from Detroit so my outlook may be different from someone in Texas. I thought about these types of things for hours. I wondered if I would have made different choices if had I been better educated before my altercation at the gas station.

A week before my trial started there was a terrible terrorist attack in Orlando. One of the terrorists actually had the same name as one of the guys I shot. I had people telling me that the negative images of Muslims may affect the jurors' decision in my favor. I really didn't know how to feel about this. Of course, I wanted to win my case, but this demonstrated my point about how we make sweeping assumptions about a group of people based off the negative or positive content we see on the media.

When one of the guys I shot left the country, I wondered, "What was he hiding? Was he even an American citizen?" I began thinking negatively of all Muslims this way. However, in the past year, after meeting people from so many different backgrounds, and reading a variety of different books, God has really given me an understanding of the context of racism and how unconscious biases can condition the minds of the masses.

At any rate, I stayed home and close to my family that weekend. My mom, dad and my girlfriend all kept my daughter active as much as possible. The goal was to keep her mind off of what was really going on. My mind was a lost cause, but at least she could feel normal.

I remember my girlfriend crying after hearing the comments my daughter continued to make. "I can't wait until you get that house daddy," she said. I was working so hard on buying my first house. However, after the financial burden of attorney fees, I had to temporarily let that dream go. *"Hopefully,"* I thought, *"after this decision on Monday, I can pick it back up again."*

Church service that morning was powerful. My entire church was praying and claiming the victory. Their faith helped increase my faith. My pastor said, "I heard the evidence in his case. If they don't make the right decision, we will protest. So get ready to bail me out. I'm not going to let them just railroad this young man!"

With Pastor Bullock, my pastor and some of the gun community backing me, I could see the streets filled with protesters. This could very easily turn into a very, very high-profile situation if things went wrong. Of course, by "wrong", I mean, not in my favor!

CHAPTER 13
The Verdict Is In

"Never have I witnessed such sincere hospitality and overwhelming spirit of true brotherhood as is practiced by people of all colors and races here in this ancient Holy Land, the home of Abraham, Muhammad and all the other Prophets of the Holy Scriptures. For the past week, I have been utterly speechless and spellbound by the graciousness I see displayed all around me by people of all colors."

– *Malcolm X, Letter from Mecca*

I'd been walking in this nightmare for over a year and it was finally coming to a head. The day was finally here. The day of the infamous verdict. I woke up that morning in shock from an adrenaline rush of fear that was building up over the Father's Day weekend. "How long will it take for the jury to make this decision? One day... two days?" I was wondering and worrying at the same time.

Ambiguity and uncertainty swept the hallways, leaving everyone stressed, scared and even physically ill – especially me. At times, I felt as if I was going to vomit on my new Hugo Boss suit. I felt vulnerable to every sound, smell and touch. Everything any person said to me that day almost brought me to tears. *"This is it!"* I thought as the words "Guilty" and "Not Guilty" ran through my head over and over again as I paced back and forth waiting to hear my fate.

My normal crew was there. My mom, dad, girlfriend, church family and friends who'd had my back since day one. I looked my girlfriend in her small, brown eyes and saw hurt and hope at the same time. Her tears and weak smile summed up this past year and a half. *"If I get out of this, I'm going to marry this girl,"* I said to myself not taking into account she may not even trust me again. At that moment, my liquor craving came back. I yelled out loud, "I need a drink!" I'm sure even my pastor could understand that considering the circumstances.

I have to say that my mom and dad were unbelievably strong. Generally, my family's demeanor was positive, but while waiting on the unpredictable jury in the antiquated courtroom, I looked towards where my mother was sitting. When I saw her almost in tears it made me realize that I wasn't the only one impacted by this situation, but my family was also. It hurt them just as much as it did me, if not more than me.

I watched everyone in the courtroom, from my friend, Josh, who took the stand on my behalf as a character witnesses earlier in the trial, to my pastor, who was probably being questioned for supporting a man who shot two people. Then, there were the older mothers of the church, whose prayer signals were stronger than a Verizon wireless connection. I appreciated everybody in that room at that moment. I felt like the world's greatest family was there in the lion's den with me.

To my surprise, the prosecutor of this case was out of town and there was a substitute prosecutor. "This is unbelievable!" I thought. "She couldn't even come to court to see the verdict of the case she fought so hard for? What could that mean? Does she think she has this thing in the bag? Or is she disappointed and felt like I might actually beat this thing?"

Then, there was the jury. I scrutinized each jury member as they walked quickly back to deliberate, leaving us in the hallway, anxious to hear their stance on the case. I tried to read their facial expressions and body language to see if I would make it out of this calamity. I was upset because I couldn't read anyone's body language. Nevertheless, somehow, my gut was telling me that the "Alpha and Omega" of the jury was the middle-aged Black woman who was a social worker for a living. She was the one taking detailed notes and asking questions throughout the trial.

In the middle of the fire it is important that you pay attention to who the leaders of the jury might be. Who is calling the shots? Signs of leadership among jurors are:

1) The member who asks the most questions. This usually means they are paying attention.
2) The member who is taking detailed notes. From my experience, women seem to take more notes than men. These notes will be what the jury will review during their deliberation.
3) The member who makes constant eye contact with you. Usually, that jury member is the one who is trying to read your body language.

While I was in deep thought, I had flashbacks of important moments in my life. I was still battling with the concept of cognitive dissonance. I sat back and wondered what my mental state would be after this. With all that I'd learned, I really believed God had a plan for me.

I'd experienced multiple cultural shocks in my life in eighteen months. I'd experienced life changing events in a short period of time. I'd grown in my discernment and understanding of life as a whole. My faith has been put through unbelievable tests. I have seen God, time and time again, get me out of situations that I shouldn't have been able to escape.

My biggest life challenge was here and, should I be absolved from all counts against me, this would propel me to the next level of leadership. One thing for sure was that I was eager to learn the truth. Through the books I've read and the people I've encountered, I was constantly in search of the truth. I believed that if God delivered me out of this situation, I would dedicate my life to finding the truth, speaking the truth and teaching the truth.

I walked the hallways wondering what was taking the jury so long to come to decision. *"Hello! We've been out here for 2 hours already,"* I wanted to stick my head in the room and remind them that Black lives mattered. The wait was driving me crazy! I wanted to know the situation that was happening inside.

"Was a member of the jury refusing to say I was innocent? Were there 11 jurors refusing to say I was innocent and stuck because one person refused to believe that I did anything but defend myself and my friend? What was

going on?!" I had to calm down.

I sat back and observed the sheriffs and other attorneys walking around in the hallway laughing and joking. I could really get a sense that this is just a job for them. They are all coworkers. In fact, it seemed like everybody was cool with each other. It's nothing to see prosecutors and defense attorneys have lunch or dinner together all of the time. When you see that as you're going through your trial, you just feel like a pawn in their game.

After waiting for over three hours, my attorney came to me and my heart stopped. I knew the decision had been made. "The verdict is in, Marcus," he said in a somber tone. My mind began racing. I suddenly started sobbing. I was a nervous wreck. This is it. This is the moment of truth.

The courtroom felt like a quiet storm. The aura of the room was a lot more stern than usual. Extra sheriffs were called to the courtroom. It was as if they needed backup just in case I, or my family, got out of control in the event of a guilty verdict. I heard the officers' ideas of what would happen in my mind, or so I thought. They probably were making bets with each other on whether or not I would get convicted and whether or not my family would act a fool if I did.

The moment I saw the jurors come back into the courtroom, a black cloud of fear came over me, but I knew if my family felt it the way I did, they would crumble. Our strength kept each other from losing it. This was a team effort, and I see the value of having family and friends that love you on this journey.

The officers surrounded me and watched my every move. I was surrounded by a wall of cops. I became claustrophobic or "officer-phobic." The last time I was surrounded by a wall of officers they had their guns out, telling me to get on the ground. With sweat on my brow and a little bit of cottonmouth, I asked my private detective who stood next to me on my left. "What's this for?" I asked already knowing the answer. "It's just procedures," he said. *"I hope they get this verdict right because this could get ugly,"* I thought to myself.

My private detective was a big part of this case. His presentation in the courtroom really made a difference. Not only was he a private detective that I hired, he also was a part of my support system. He was a neat, 50-something guy with short gray hair and a nicely trimmed beard. His suit looked like he could have gotten it from Steve Harvey himself. His gold watch and cufflinks would always match and he would usually wear a purple or pink bow tie that would offset the dark colors of his blazer and shirt. He had a great deal of information and knowledge about the justice system. I respected him very much.

As each juror took their seat, the judge began to read out the rules. He explained that the bailiff would be the one who would read each charge (all seven of them), along with the jurors' decision. It was obvious to me at this point that it wasn't a hung jury so whatever the decision was the team of jurors were all in agreeance.

I looked at them all in their eyes and then calmly looked down. It is also important to note that staring too long in the eyes of jurors is a sign of intimidation and can be looked at as juror intimidation. I spoke to myself in my head, "This is it, Marcus. It's time for the decision. It's time to face this monster. It's time to get my life back. I'm ready. I'm ready. I'm ready!"

The bailiff read the first account. "Count One, assault with intent to murder, punishable by life or any number of years. The jury finds the defendant... not guilty."

The pressure of that one "not guilty" made my heart skip a beat. I heard my family start crying in the background. As much as I wanted to, I couldn't turn around and make eye contact. Any look they gave me would have destroyed me emotionally. I could only wonder how many people have heart attacks in this place.

The bailiff continued, "Count Two, assault with intent to murder, possible by life or any number of years. The jury finds the defendant... not guilty."

I heard more crying from the back. I wanted to turn around and say, *"We still have five counts to go! Get it together family!"* I was so nervous that I couldn't cry. I knew the fight wasn't over yet. I needed to be stronger than ever before.

The bailiff went on, "Count Three, assault with intent to do great bodily harm less than murder punishable by a maximum of 10 years. The jury finds the defendant... not guilty."

"Okay, this is killing me," I thought, anxiously. We are already three accounts in and I still can't celebrate! *"Why won't they just read them all together really, really fast?"* I wondered to myself. *"Dragging this out will make anyone faint!"*

The bailiff resumed, "Count Four, intent to do great bodily harm less than murder, punishable by maximum of ten years. The jury finds the defendant... not guilty."

By this time, my tears were rolling, uncontrollably, down my face. I could no longer hold it in. If there was a time to cry or show emotion, this was the time to let it out. Nonetheless I was still strong. I still had my head high, but my face was like Niagara Falls.

"Count Five," the bailiff proceeded, "Assault with a dangerous weapon punishable by a maximum of four years. The jury finds the defendant... not guilty."

After this count was read, there was a different emotion I noticed in one of the jurors. Never before had any of them really shown any emotional signs until now. One of them, a young Black girl, looked at me with a facial expression I'll never forget. There was a calmness in her face that offered some reassurance that everything was going to be okay. It's hard for me to describe this look, but it was almost as if, without saying anything, without doing anything, without winking, without smiling, she was letting me know that everything was going to be alright. The burden was lifted, God had already told me. It's over!

"Count Six, assault with a dangerous weapon punishable by maximum of 4 years. The jury finds the defendant... not guilty."

"And Count Seven," the bailiff prepared to conclude his reading, "Weapons felony firearm, mandatory 2 years consecutively with preceding any term of imprisonment imposed for the felony or attempted felony conviction. The jury finds the defendant... not guilty."

My legs were weak, but my spirit was strong! The entire courtroom almost exploded into tears of joy and thankfulness to God. "Order! Order in the Court!" the judge yelled. You cannot show any emotion in his courtroom even after being exonerated from all charges. It's like you're not allowed to be human. The judge asked the jury members one by one if they agreed with the decision and if they were influenced in any way by anyone. They agreed unanimously.

I turned to my left and right to shake the hands of my attorney and my private detective. The judge then said, "Step out, wait for your paperwork. You may talk to the jurors as they leave court." In my mind I was thinking about, *"What if I took that plea bargain? I would have missed freedom!"*

With sweaty palms and a heavy arm, I shook Mr. Craig's hand, looked him in the eye and said, "I made it out the lion's den." I stuck to my guns (how ironic!) and to my faith, even though it was an emotional roller coaster.

As we left out of the courtroom, we quickly greeted the jurors. They all hugged me and some shook my hand. This was the most emotional time you will ever see a group of strangers be. All week we had to walk past these people and not acknowledge them. Now, we can talk and ask exactly what happened in there!

Each of the jurors seemed like he or she was rooting for me from the beginning. Just by the comments they were sharing, I feel like they had already made the decision from the start. The older Black lady said to me, "Now you can go enjoy your Father's Day with your daughter." The white guy, who was the engineered that I liked, said, "Hey man, it was a unanimous decision."

Then, the one juror, who made eye contact with me while I was on the stand, said something that really stuck with me. "I know it's going to be hard to get your life back on track, but I'm praying for you and your family. Continue being a great father to your daughter. You have a testimony. Use it to help others," she said, encouraging me.

The discernment and passion in her voice sent chills down my spine. I felt as if she knew that I had a calling in life. She only saw me in my darkest hour, but she must have seen something in me that made her connect with me like that.

I was inspired by some of these jurors. When you have strangers rooting for you, it makes you have a whole new look on life! If I saw any of them today at a restaurant I would pay for their meal immediately with no hesitation. These people saved my life.

My girlfriend leaped into my arms crying and I was almost tackled and dog piled by the rest of my family. Minutes later, a sheriff walked up to me and shook my hand.

"You take care of your mother. I can tell you have a good one. She will go above and beyond for you."

This brings me back to the importance of having family at your side. The sheriff could see that I came from good stock. He witnessed my mother's involvement in my life, along with my father and so many church members and friends. This positive support in the courtroom sets a positive context for the jury.

Everyone in the courtroom on my behalf had a part in me being exonerated. The image that was painted showed I had good character and, even though we had the facts and evidence to win the case, remember demonstrating good character is sometimes enough to exonerate you by itself.

I walked through the hallways and down the escalators with tears of joy as my attorney handed me paperwork to prove my innocence. I had to take the documents to the tether office to remove my dreaded ankle jewelry. "You did good on the stand, Marcus! No doubt, you're one of the best clients that I've had," he said. There was a lot of pressure on him to win this case. Even though the media didn't show back up to hear the verdict, this still was a big case for him to win.

As I walked out of the court house, I observed so many others who were still on trial. Some families were crying and screaming that their loved ones didn't get the same outcome as I had. I saw others walking in through the metal detectors with their new-found friend on their ankle. I'm sure they were praying for a similar outcome as mine, no doubt.

Sheriffs were waiving the metal detecting wands up and down people's legs, almost violating them. German shepherd dogs were barking when they smelled something or saw something suspicious. That building is something that I never wanted to come back to, nor did I want to see any of my friends end up there.

There was still work to be done. I needed to make it from the courthouse to the other jail to get my tether removed. I'd never been so happy to go to the tether office in my life! This was the first time I went down there with a smile. I was hoping the process was quick because I was ready to go home to see my daughter and give her a hug and let her know her daddy was coming home and staying home!

It didn't take long for me to get the device removed. As a matter of fact, it was much easier than getting it on. The process was simple. After a couple of snips and clips and I was officially a free man. A couple of officers looked shocked to see the paperwork say "Exonerated of seven felonies". This doesn't happen often.

This time around, as an innocent man, everybody was super friendly. What a difference a "not guilty" verdict can have on public perception. When you're a labeled a criminal, you're treated like one. When you're labeled innocent, you're treated like a free, law-abiding citizen once again. Labels matter. We can't ignore them. They are real, they mean something and people react to them.

I posted the good news on Facebook and my inbox filled with "Congratulations!" and "Thank God!" messages. I made calls to those who were close to me, but just couldn't make it to court. My family and I went out to a nearby steak house where we had dinner for the first time in a while in a good mood. Afterwards, we headed back to house and, along the way, we picked up my daughter.

She was at a relative's house while we finished out in court. I looked at her and smiled. I held her with convoluted emotions running through me like kids on a playground. I didn't know what to say to her. "Daddy is done with the ankle box," I said. It was all I could think of at that moment. She smiled and said, "Now you can get in the pool and leave the house?"

I couldn't do anything but laugh. I thanked God for this moment. All the postponements of hearings and protracting of this open and shut case was the most hellish experience of my life. Now it was over and I could go back to being a father, not just another young, Black man being crushed by the criminal justice system.

A lot could have happened with me. I could have been killed at the gas station by the man who was bothering my friend. I could have been killed by the police once they found me. I could have completely lost my mind while I was in jail. All of those moments mattered and, going through that hell, I've learned a great deal about who I am and who I want to be.

Later that day, after getting a haircut, I came home to rest. I was emotionally drained. Somehow I felt tired and energetic at the same time. My daughter, who never left my side, looked just as worn out as I was looking. I finally had a minute to lay down. Then, I heard knock at the door.

My daughter, who can be "Curious George" at times, looked out of the window. "Daddy! Daddy!" she yelled. "There is a man and lady with a camera outside!" I looked at her with a confused look on my face. Who would be outside with cameras? I walked to the window and, to my surprise, she was right.

On the other side of my door was one of my favorite news anchors to watch, Taryn Asher, and a camera man accompanying her. I hesitantly opened the door and wondered how they found me and, more importantly, what they wanted.

"Hello, Marcus! Taryn Asher with Fox 2 News. We heard the great news on the verdict. Could we get statement from you?" I could tell that Fox 2 News was anxious to get the first crack at the story. The shooting Santa Claus was found "Not Guilty". What I remember from previous experiences, once one station gets the story, others want the exclusive as well.

With the camera in my face and mic to my mouth. I paused for three seconds and finally said, "Can you give me a few minutes? I'm a little tired." The journey was not over for Marcus Weldon. This was just beginning!

APPENDIX

Authors and Books that Influenced Me

On house arrest, you don't have much of anything to do, but get into trouble or read. I even started reading the Constitution and the Bill of Rights because I was trying to figure out the law. You have to find something to be productive. Here are some authors and books I read that helped me.

1. Cornel West - Race Matters
2. Kevin Boyle - Arc of Justice
3. Dr. Michael Arnheim - U.S. Constitution for Dummies
4. Malcolm Gladwell - The Outliers
5. Malcom Gladwell -The Tipping Point
6. Robert Greene - 33 Strategies of War
7. Michelle Alexander - The New Jim Crow
8. Booker T. Washington - Up From Slavery
9. John Hope Bryant - How the Poor Can Save Capitalism
10. Carter G. Woodson - The Mis-Education of the Negro
11. Reverend Kenn Blanchard - Black Man with a Gun
12. Ron Paul - The School Revolution: A New Answer for our Broken Education System
13. Shaka Senghor - Writing My Wrongs: Life, Death

and Redemption in an American Prison
14. Robbin Shipp, Esq. and Nick Chiles - Justice While Black: Helping African-American families Navigate and Survive the Criminal Justice System

Mug shot / Speedway Gas station: scene of the shooting.

Face down, in the infamous Santa suit, surrounded by police. Image captured by a bystander on cell phone.

Dr. Cornell West

CJ Grisham, 2nd Amendment Advocate

Dr. Umar Johnson

Church member, Dee Bradfield, holds my hand as I fight for my freedom.

Support on Twitter as discussed in Chapter 8

www.ingramcontent.com/pod-product-compliance
Lightning Source LLC
Chambersburg PA
CBHW070546010526
44118CB00012B/1247